TURKEY'S SOUTHERN SHORE

By the same author

AEGEAN TURKEY

AN ARCHAEOLOGICAL GUIDE

Frontispiece: The Lycian mountains from Antalya

TURKEY'S SOUTHERN SHORE
AN ARCHAEOLOGICAL GUIDE

GEORGE E. BEAN

LONDON
ERNEST BENN LIMITED

First published 1968 by Ernest Benn Limited
Bouverie House · Fleet Street · London · EC4

Distributed in Canada by
The General Publishing Company Limited · Toronto

© *George E. Bean 1968*

Printed in Great Britain

510–03251–6

Foreword

CERTAIN critics of my earlier book *Aegean Turkey*, which dealt with the ancient cities of the west coast, complained that it might with advantage have been extended further to the south, and expressed a hope that this defect might be remedied in the future. The present work offers a partial answer, and may be considered as a companion volume to the other. It deals with those places which are within comfortable reach of Antalya on the south coast. This region is very rich in remains of antiquity, but there is really very little to help the English-speaking traveller to enjoy and understand them. The accounts of the early explorers, Beaufort, Spratt and Forbes, Fellows and others, are still fascinating to read, but are no longer adequate today. More recently Freya Stark has travelled in these parts, and in her *Alexander's Path* has given her impressions of them. Otherwise there is hardly anything for the English reader outside the learned journals.[1]

I have used the same mode of treatment as in *Aegean Turkey*, but readers of that book will notice a considerable difference here. Whereas the west-coast cities teem with famous names, and the anecdotes of writers like Herodotus, Pausanias and Aelius Aristides bring the ancient cities to life for us, the south coast is comparatively neglected by the ancient authors. It is safe to say that of all the cities dealt with in this book not one ever produced a single citizen whose name is known to any but specialists. Consequently the ruins have for the most part to speak for themselves; luckily they are in general well able to do so.

Antalya has in recent years developed greatly as a summer resort. The roads to the north and east are very much improved, and Antalya itself, Side and Alânya now possess good hotels. Spring and autumn are the best seasons for a visit; the middle of the summer is distinctly hot, and the winter tends

[1] Since the above was written I have seen Gwyn Williams' *Turkey*, where the reader will find a (necessarily brief) account of most of the cities I deal with here.

7

to be rainy, though not cold. Excavation on the south coast
has only begun. Side has been transformed since 1947 by the
excellent work of the Archaeological Department of Istanbul
University, and digging has now started at Perge; otherwise
nothing has been done.

I have myself visited within the last two years all the places
treated in this book; the descriptions are therefore at first
hand. At the same time I am heavily indebted—as all must
be who make a study of these ruins—to Lanckoronski's *Städte
Pamphyliens und Pisidiens*, which is still the standard work
on the subject; and in Chapters 6 and 7 I have borrowed
freely from Seton Lloyd's and Storm Rice's *Alânya* and A. M.
Mansel's *Die Ruinen von Side*. To these writers I offer my
grateful acknowledgments. The photographs were taken by
me; the sketches in the text are by my wife.

In speaking of theatres, stadia, gymnasia and other buildings, much of what I wrote in *Aegean Turkey* could have been
repeated here, but this I have mostly avoided doing; it is
irksome to write the same thing twice, and no less so to read it
twice. The other book is always available for those who are
interested. As before, my lower limit of time is in general
about A.D. 300, but I have made an inevitable exception in the
case of Alânya and, to a lesser extent, of Antalya.

I am conscious that (as was said by critics of *Aegean Turkey*)
the title of this book seems to promise more than is actually provided. It is true that not all the south coast is covered. For this
I ask the reader's indulgence, and his patience: I hope, if I am
spared, to do something before long to repair the deficiency.

For the Turkish names I have again used the modern
Turkish spelling. In this (to repeat for convenience) the vowels
are pronounced as in German, the consonants as in English,
with these exceptions: c = English j; ç = English (t)ch; ş =
English sh; ğ after soft vowels = English y, after hard vowels
it merely lengthens them. The dotless ı is a sound not unlike
the indeterminate vowel-sound in 'bor*ough*' or '*again*'. In
speaking Turkish names the stress should be spread more
evenly over the syllables than is done in English.

Contents

9

List of Plates

[*In one section between pages* 48 *and* 49]

11

List of Illustrations in Text

15

Glossary

Agora. Market-place; the civic centre of the city and general place of resort.

Archaic period. Approximately the seventh and sixth centuries B.C.

Ashlar masonry. Walls of rectangular blocks laid in horizontal courses.

Cavea. Auditorium of a theatre.

Cella. The main chamber of a temple, where the cult-statue stood.

Classical Greek period. Approximately the fifth and fourth centuries B.C.

Corinthian order. The latest of the three main orders, especially favoured in Roman times. The characteristic feature of the order is the capital, consisting of a drum adorned with sprays of acanthus leaves. Otherwise similar to the Ionic order.

Diazoma. Passage dividing the cavea of a theatre horizontally.

Doric order. The severest of the three orders, very frequently used in Greece, much more rarely in Asia Minor. The columns stand directly on the platform, without any base, and have normally twenty flutes. The capitals are of 'inverted Eton collar' shape.

Hellenistic period. The period from Alexander the Great to Augustus—approximately the last three centuries B.C.

Ionic order. The style most frequently used in the temples of Asia Minor. The columns stand on moulded bases and have normally twenty-four flutes. The chief characteristic is the capitals, which have 'ram's horns' volutes at either side.

Nymphaeum. A decorative installation for the supply of water to the citizens.

Orchestra. The dance-floor in a theatre, between the stage-building and the cavea; used in classical times by the chorus, later occupied by seats for distinguished spectators.

17

Parodoi. Open passages in a theatre, between the stage-building and the retaining-walls of the cavea, used for the entrance and exit of chorus and spectators.

Proscenium. That part of a stage-building which projects in front into the orchestra; used as a stage in post-classical times.

Stadium. (1) A measure of length, about 180 metres, but variable. (2) A foot-race of this length. (3) The arena in which foot-races and other athletic events took place.

Stele. A slab of stone set upright and generally bearing writing or decoration or both.

Stoa. Covered portico beside a street or agora or elsewhere.

Vomitorium. Covered passage in a Roman theatre, affording entrance and exit for the spectators.

PART ONE

Introduction

CHAPTER ONE

Historical

THE SOUTH COAST of Asia Minor falls naturally into four
distinct and sharply contrasting geographical regions. At the
east end is the fertile plain of Adana, Tarsus and Mersin,
known in antiquity as Smooth Cilicia; this is now, by virtue of
its cotton harvests, one of the richest districts of Turkey. To
the west of this is the utterly different Rough Cilicia; here the
Taurus mountains approach the coast, their southern slopes
cut up by deep river valleys plunging down in tremendous
gorges for thousands of feet—scenically magnificent country,
but poor and productive of little besides timber. Further to the
west the mountains gradually recede, and from the neighbourhood of Manavgat to that of Antalya the coast is bordered by
an extensive plain, the ancient Pamphylia, something over
fifty miles long. Well watered by three good-sized rivers and
numerous streams, this plain also produces cotton as its main
crop. In Greek and Roman times it supported five large cities,
Attaleia, Perge, Sillyum, Aspendus and Side. To the west again
the country changes once more and becomes as mountainous
and inhospitable as it is to the east. This is the ancient Lycia,
the land of tombs. Like Rough Cilicia, it produces abundant
timber and little else. To the north of the Pamphylian plain
the mountains rise more gradually to the highlands of Pisidia
around Burdur, Isparta and Beyşehir.

Surrounded in this way by mountains, and lying aside from
the main east-west land routes, Pamphylia played a comparatively minor part in the history of Anatolia. How things
were in the second millennium B.C. we cannot know till the
geography of the Hittite period is more definitively established;
the Greek history of the region begins, here as elsewhere, at the
time of the Trojan War. Troy fell, as was believed, in 1184 B.C.

and this date is probably not far wrong; following the capture, a strong tradition said that a 'mixed multitude' of people wandered across Asia to Pamphylia, where most of them settled; some, however, moved on to Cilicia. As leaders of this migration the historians record the three famous seers Mopsus, Calchas and Amphilochus. All was not harmony, for we hear of the settlers warring with each other—and even in later times relations between Aspendus and Side, for example, were frequently strained. The legends varied in detail; some said that Calchas never reached Pamphylia at all, having died of mortification at Claros when defeated by Mopsus in a contest of divination;[1] on the other hand, he is recorded at Perge among the city's founders.[2] Mopsus and Amphilochus are said to have passed on into Cilicia, where after founding the city of Mallus they quarrelled and killed each other in single combat.

Pamphylia is one of the few countries of Asia Minor that have a Greek name, the 'land of all tribes'. It is natural to suppose that this name derives from the 'mixed multitude' of settlers; but the Greek fondness for inventing 'eponymous' founders led some to assert that it was given by Mopsus in honour either of his daughter Pamphylia or of his half-sister Pamphyle. Pliny, on the other hand, says that Pamphylia was formerly called Mopsopia. These assertions may safely be disregarded.

Normally the Greek traditions concerning these early times must be taken with great reserve; but the legend of the settlement of Pamphylia, especially as it relates to Mopsus, is in fact confirmed in its main outlines by independent evidence. In the first place, the Pamphylian dialect of Greek, as revealed by coins and inscriptions, bears a close resemblance to the language spoken in southern Greece before the invasion of the Dorians. These invaders arrived within a century after the Trojan War, overran most of Greece and permanently occupied the Peloponnese, bringing a new language with them. The Greek settlers in Pamphylia must therefore have left Greece before about 1100 B.C., and may well have arrived, as the tradition said, soon after the fall of Troy. In any case, the early settlement of the country by Greeks is confirmed.

Secondly, Mopsus' existence as a historical personage, and

---

[1] *Aegean Turkey*, p. 191.   [2] Below, p. 53 and Fig. 6.

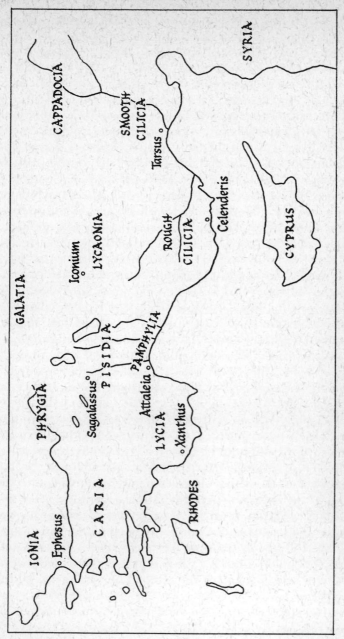

Fig. 1 Districts of Southern Asia Minor

23

his association with Pamphylia, are proved in an interesting way by Hittite documents recently discovered. On the early city site at Karatepe in eastern Cilicia were found two versions of a long inscription, one in Phoenician and the other in Hittite hieroglyphs; in this the king Asitawandas records his foundation of the city. He describes himself as a descendant of an ancestor whose name is given in the Phoenician as MPS and in the Hittite as Muksas. These texts date to the eighth century, but Mopsus also occurs much earlier than this on a Hittite cuneiform tablet in the form Muksus; this establishes his date as around 1200 B.C., which agrees well with the Greek tradition. Now Mopsus was said to have founded the city of Aspendus, and the name of this city appears on its early coins as Estwediiys; the similarity of this to that of Asitawa(n)das must be more than coincidence, and we may fairly assume that Aspendus was called after an earlier Asitawandas, this name, like Mopsus itself, being recurrent in the family.

We may therefore with some confidence accept the Greek tradition of the settlement under Mopsus and others soon after the fall of Troy. The Pamphylian cities themselves had no doubt on the matter; Mopsus was expressly honoured as a founder (with others) at Perge.[1] And in the inscriptions of Cilicia, down to the time of the Roman empire, the name Mopsus is often borne by private individuals.

Reference was made above to the Pamphylian dialect of Greek. Our knowledge of this is derived principally from a single long inscription carved on the doorpost of a building at Sillyum[2] dating to about 200 B.C. Coins and inscriptions of similar date at Perge and Aspendus, consisting of little more than proper names, show similar peculiarities of form and spelling; it is therefore clear that a dialect common to these three cities continued to be spoken down to the second century B.C. Side on the other hand is in different case. The earliest Sidetan coins and inscriptions use a language and alphabet peculiar to that city and not yet deciphered. More will be said of this later.[3] Following Alexander's conquests the use of standard Greek, known as the *koine*, spread over Asia Minor and the local dialects gradually disappeared.

[1] Below, pp. 45, 53.   [2] Below, p. 63.   [3] Below, pp. 78–9.

For the next five or six hundred years after the settlement the history of Pamphylia is a total blank. In the course of the sixth century the kings of Lydia were busy in extending their empire over western Asia, and the last of them, Croesus, finally subdued it all, with the exception of the Lycians and Cilicians, whose wild and mountainous countries would not repay the trouble of conquest. But the Lydian domination was short-lived. In 546 B.C. Croesus was disastrously defeated by the Persian king Cyrus, and Persian dominion replaced the Lydian.

The story of the Persian Wars, and the attempts by Darius in 490 B.C. and by Xerxes ten years later to invade and subjugate Greece, is familiar. Xerxes' army, estimated by Herodotus at the fabulous figure of 1,700,000 men, was drawn from all parts of his empire, and the Pamphylians were not excluded. They were equipped, says Herodotus, in Greek fashion, and contributed thirty ships to the Persian fleet. The historian notes that they were the descendants of the settlers under Calchas and Amphilochus; they were thus fighting against their own kinsmen. The Carian queen Artemisia, whose advice was highly esteemed by Xerxes, warned him that the Pamphylians were worthless allies; indeed it is likely that their heart was not in the business. In the actual campaign we hear nothing of their performance.

The utter defeat of the Persians at Salamis and Plataea (479 B.C.) left Athens in complete control of the Aegean shores, and a league was at once formed under Athenian leadership which included nearly all the cities and towns, Greek and barbarian, on the west coast of Asia Minor. The professed purpose of this league, called the Delian League, was to prevent the recurrence of the Persian menace, and the members were required to furnish either money or ships with this object. The south-coast cities of Lycia, Pamphylia and Cilicia were not at first included, but continued for the most part to be held by Persian garrisons; and Xerxes, in a final effort at resistance, had by 469 B.C. collected a large army and fleet at Aspendus. In that year the Athenian general Cimon led a brilliantly successful expedition to those parts. He won over or coerced the cities of Caria and Lycia held by the Persians, then attacked the assembled enemy forces at the mouth of the river

Eurymedon. The sea-battle, long and sternly contested, ended in an Athenian victory, and many of the Persian ships fell into Cimon's hands. Thereupon he decided, as night was falling, to go on and attack the enemy's land forces. His own force of marines was, of course, vastly outnumbered, so he resorted to a stratagem: dressing the best of his men in tiaras and other Persian garb taken from his prisoners, he put them on board the captured Persian vessels and sent them to land at the river-mouth. The Persian soldiers, duly deceived, accepted them as friends, and the camp was soon in complete confusion; Cimon followed up with the rest of his men, and a second victory was quickly won. Such a double victory by land and sea in a single day was claimed as a record, and was celebrated at Athens by a dedicatory monument; its practical effect was that the Persian peril was finally eliminated, and that the cities of the south coast (or some of them) were enrolled in the Athenian league. Whether they were pleased by the change is doubtful; there is no actual evidence that they ever paid any contribution to the league funds.[1]

Freedom from Persia lasted for less than a century. In 431 B.C. began the long Peloponnesian War between Athens and Sparta. When this ended in 404 with the defeat of Athens the Athenian league was inherited by the victors. But the Spartans soon showed themselves quite incapable of managing an overseas empire, and before long the Persians were active again in Asia Minor; by 386 B.C. the Greeks were reduced to signing a peace with the Great King by the terms of which all the Asiatic cities were recognised as belonging to him.

How this affected Pamphylia in particular we have little evidence to determine. The country was placed under a regional governor called a satrap, whose main duty was to see that tribute and taxes were duly paid; otherwise the Persian government seems to have been very easy-going. Aspendus and Side were permitted to issue their own coinage—as indeed they had done under the former Persian dominion in the early fifth century.

This second period of Persian rule lasted till the coming of

[1] See Appendix I.

Alexander the Great. In 334 B.C. the young Macedonian king crossed into Asia with the avowed intent to crush the Persian power and so avenge the wrongs formerly inflicted on Greece. Following his first victory at the river Granicus he advanced into Lydia and Ionia unopposed by any large army; most of the cities, defended only by their own garrisons, submitted to him without resistance, though one or two, notably Miletus and Halicarnassus, gave him considerable trouble to capture. In the following winter he passed on into Lycia without opposition, accepting the surrender of the individual towns, and in early spring arrived in Pamphylia.

His first halt was at Perge; Attaleia was not yet in existence. The Pergaeans were already friendly to him and had previously served him in Lycia as guides. Advancing from here he was met on the road by envoys from Aspendus offering to surrender their city, but asking that no Macedonian garrison be left in it. Alexander agreed, but required them to contribute to his army fifty talents in money[1] and the horses which they had been in the habit of furnishing as tribute to the Persian king. The Aspendian envoys accepted the conditions and Alexander moved on to Side. Meeting with no opposition here, he left a garrison in the town and marched back to Sillyum. Here for for the first time he found himself resisted. The place, says the historian, was naturally strong and was defended in the Persian cause by a mixed force of foreign mercenaries and native barbarians. Alexander's hastily improvised assault was unsuccessful, and before another could be mounted unsatisfactory news arrived from Aspendus. The Aspendians had refused to ratify the terms agreed by their ambassadors; instead, they had brought all their property inside the city, repaired the weak places in the walls, shut their gates in the faces of Alexander's envoys, and prepared to defend themselves. Alexander at once abandoned Sillyum and marched with his full force to Aspendus, where he occupied the lower town and surrounded the acropolis. The Aspendians then suddenly lost their nerve; they seem not to have expected that Alexander, having once passed back to the west, would come in person to attack them. At all events they now offered to

---

[1] Perhaps something like £50,000 in modern terms.

submit on the terms already agreed. Alexander might well have accepted; the place was a strong one, and the last thing he wanted was a long siege. Nevertheless he demanded in addition an extra fifty talents, hostages from the most influential citizens, and the payment of an annual tribute to Macedon. The Aspendians could only agree.

Alexander's purpose in overrunning these parts was to deny the south coast as a naval base to the Persians. With the occupation of Aspendus and Side he regarded this as sufficiently accomplished and made no attempt on Rough Cilicia. Sillyum was not a maritime city, having no river like Perge or Aspendus, and was not worth the trouble of a siege; he therefore made no further assault upon it, but returned at once to Perge. It was now time for him to make his way northwards into Phrygia, where he had a rendezvous at Gordium with the other part of his army under his officer Parmenio. 'His road', says the historian,[1] 'led past the city of Termessus.' Now, this was by no means the easiest way to Phrygia, nor the shortest, and it involved the passage of a narrow defile defended by the hostile Termessians. One wonders why he did not take the natural route followed approximately by the modern highroad to Burdur. Perhaps, as Freya Stark suggests, his Pergaean advisers misled him, being very ready that the Termessians should be suppressed. At all events, after a brush with the defenders at the narrows he was contemplating a siege of Termessus when envoys arrived from the city of Selge professing friendship; Alexander received them kindly and took them into his confidence. What they said to him we do not hear; possibly they pointed out to him that he was on the wrong road; in any case, he at once abandoned the idea of besieging Termessus and made straight for Sagalassus.

Alexander's subsequent conquest of the Persian empire, followed by his early death at Babylon (323 B.C.), at once changed the face of the eastern world and left it without a ruler. The power that would have been his passed to the hands

[1] Our authority for this campaign is Arrian, who wrote in the second century A.D. an account of Alexander's conquest of Persia based on the work of Ptolemy, one of his generals and afterwards king of Egypt.

of his generals, who spent the next forty years fighting one another for the newly conquered territories. By the end of that time three main kingdoms were established: first Greece and Macedonia; second, Egypt under Ptolemy and his successors, all of whom took the name Ptolemy; and third, Syria under the Seleucid dynasty, whose kings were called either Seleucus or Antiochus. To these a fourth was added after 280 B.C. with the rise of the Attalid dynasty at Pergamum; its kings bore the names Attalus and Eumenes.

Of these kingdoms Pamphylia would naturally be expected to belong to the Seleucids, and the existence of a city of Seleuceia at its eastern extremity (in addition to the greater Seleuceia in Cilicia further east) testifies to their temporary control of at least a part of it. At the same time it was claimed by the Ptolemies as among their possessions, and this claim, too, has evidence to support it. The geographer Strabo mentions a city of Ptolemais, otherwise utterly unknown, which he places in Pamphylia; but it evidently lay well to the east of the river Melas (the Manavgat Çayı) and so in what is more usually regarded as Rough Cilicia. An inscription of the third century B.C. found at Aspendus confers citizenship on certain soldiers for their services to King Ptolemy, probably Ptolemy I. But in fact it seems that neither Seleucid nor Ptolemaic control was ever much more than nominal, and the cities were in effect independent.

At least, this seems clearly to have been the case towards the end of the third century. In 223 B.C. the youthful Antiochus III came to the throne of Syria, and shortly afterwards sent his uncle, by name Achaeus, to recover Asia Minor from the king of Pergamum, into whose hands it had fallen. This Achaeus successfully did, but was thereupon persuaded to renounce his loyalty to his nephew and proclaim himself an independent king, which dignity he contrived to maintain for some five or six years. During this time it happened that the men of Ped-nelissus, being besieged by the men of Selge, appealed to Achaeus for help.[1] Achaeus gladly agreed and sent his lieutenant Garsyeris with an army. With the object not only of raising the siege but of rallying support to Achaeus, Garsyeris

[1] For these events see below, pp. 140–42.

marched to Perge and from there made overtures to the individual cities. Aspendus was among those who sent contingents, but the men of Side, 'partly from goodwill to Antiochus, but more from hatred of the Aspendians', declined to respond. There is no trace here of Seleucid or Ptolemaic dominion; the cities act freely and on their own initiative.

Twenty years later, however, Antiochus determined to bring the south coast firmly under his control. Cilicia and Pamphylia were occupied without apparent difficulty; but Antiochus, an energetic and ambitious monarch, finally overreached himself, and by interference in the affairs of Greece brought the Roman armies into Asia against him. Defeated in 190 B.C. in the crucial battle of Magnesia (now Manisa), where Pamphylians fought on his side, he was deprived of all his possessions north of the Taurus. Pamphylia thus remained, at least nominally, in his power, and in 188 we hear that he was maintaining a garrison at Perge; but Antiochus was in effect a spent force and he died in 187.

It was only reluctantly that the Romans had sent their legions across the Aegean; after the victory of Magnesia, having no desire to annex territory in Asia Minor, they gave most of it to Eumenes, king of Pergamum. But before withdrawing they sent an army under the consul Manlius Vulso with the professed purpose of punishing the Galatians, who lived in central Anatolia and had been allies of Antiochus. Manlius, however, turned his assignment into a reconnaissance and money-raising expedition. Instead of making at once for Galatia he turned south through Caria. On the road he was approached by envoys from Isinda, whose city was being besieged by the Termessians, with an appeal for help; accepting readily, he raised the siege and exacted a penalty of fifty talents from Termessus. Advancing into Pamphylia, he levied the same amount from Aspendus and the other cities, presumably as 'protection-money' and the price of freedom. He then turned northwards and Pamphylia was left in peace for thirty years.

Pisidia was among the districts allotted after Magnesia to Eumenes of Pergamum. Selge, however, the most powerful and warlike of the Pisidian cities, was unwilling to accept the

status of a subject and was perpetually in arms against the
Pergamene kings. In or about 158 B.C. Eumenes' successor
Attalus II embarked on a campaign to subdue the recalcitrant
city; in this he failed, but he was successful in overrunning at
least a part of Pamphylia. He was obliged to proceed with
caution, for the Pamphylian cities, having purchased their
freedom from Manlius, were protégés of Rome, and it was
Attalus' constant policy to do nothing without Roman ap-
proval. He could not therefore simply annex the ports of
Pamphylia; on the other hand, a port on the south coast was
the principal advantage of possessing the country. Attalus was
accordingly constrained to found a new harbour-town, which
he called after himself Attaleia, the modern Antalya.

In 133 B.C. Attalus III, last king of Pergamum, died and
bequeathed his kingdom to Rome. The Romans, still none too
willing to burden themselves with eastern territory, gave away
the outlying portions of the kingdom, but organised the core
of it as the Roman province of Asia. This comprised the whole
of the west-coast regions, but Lycia, Pamphylia and Cilicia
were not included. The Romans, in fact, were not much interested in the south coast, until their attention was forcibly
drawn to it by the activities of the pirates.

Rough Cilicia was perfect country for piracy and brigandage.
Its wild and almost impenetrable character rendered the rob-
bers safe from pursuit; the numerous tiny anchorages and
occasional offshore islets afforded admirable lurking-places,
and the important sea-route from Syria to the Aegean and the
west led naturally along this coast. It is not surprising that
piracy in these parts had been a problem since the fifth century
and with the gradual weakening of the Seleucid power it had
during the course of the second century grown to be a serious
menace. The Romans at first did nothing to suppress it; on the
contrary they even indirectly encouraged it, for a particular
reason. Among the most profitable forms of piracy was the
trade in slaves, and slaves were in enormous demand in Italy,
both for the houses of the upper classes in Rome and for the
farms in the country. After 167 B.C. the Romans declared
the island of Delos a free port, and at once a vast slave em-
porium was established there; the turnover, as Strabo tells us,

ran to tens of thousands in a day. But as time went on and the pirates were found to be interfering with commerce between Rome and the east, and were even venturing to harry the coasts of the province of Asia, some action became imperative. In 102 B.C. a certain Marcus Antonius, grandfather of the famous Mark Antony, was appointed with a fleet to deal with them; he succeeded in inflicting a defeat on them and seizing some of their ships. The pirates later had their revenge on him by capturing his daughter; and in general Antonius' campaign had little lasting effect.

The next Roman move was to appeal to the various friendly kings and free cities in the east to do their best to keep the seas clear for peaceful passage, but this, too—perhaps hardly surprisingly—produced little or no result. About this time also (the exact date is disputed) the Romans established a province of Cilicia. This, however, did not at first include any part of Cilicia itself, Rough or Smooth, but comprised chiefly Pamphylia, with perhaps some of the country to the north and north-west. Its name was due to its purpose, the suppression of piracy, for the word 'Cilician' had come in popular speech to mean 'pirate'.

The earliest governors were unfortunately ineffective or worse, particularly the notorious Dolabella, who regarded his province mainly as a means of enriching himself; his extortions were so outrageous that at the end of his term of office he was prosecuted at Rome and actually convicted. Such convictions were rare, for the jury was composed of politicians who might one day be governors of provinces themselves, and might well hope for indulgence towards any shortcomings of their own. Perhaps even worse than Dolabella was his subordinate Verres, who was later prosecuted by Cicero himself. This man, with Dolabella's connivance, was guilty of the most barefaced robbery, commandeering the produce of the country, or rather cash payments in lieu, and plundering the statues and votive offerings from the temples of Perge and Aspendus. These men were no doubt unusually bad examples, but in general the majority of governors under the republic saw in their province a source of profit for themselves.

In 88 B.C. Mithridates VI, king of Pontus, invaded the

Roman province in an attempt to oust the Romans from Asia. At first all went well for him, and for some time he was virtually master of all Asia Minor. To bring the south-coast regions under control he sent his lieutenants, but he does not appear to have visited these parts himself, except for a brief and unsuccessful attempt to reduce the city of Patara in Lycia. Nor was he altogether unopposed elsewhere; it is likely that Termessus suffered some damage from taking the Roman part against him.[1] Eventually he was completely defeated by Pompey the Great and expelled from Asia.

Meanwhile the pirates flourished unchecked, and not only in Cilicia but also on the west coast of the gulf of Antalya, where a pirate chief by the name of Zenicetes had strongly established himself as virtual ruler of the country. His headquarters was at the city of Olympus, which had formerly belonged to the Lycian League and had presumably been forcibly captured by him.

Effective action was eventually undertaken by Rome with the appointment in 78 B.C. as governor of Cilicia of Servilius Vatia, a contrast in every way to Dolabella. He first defeated the pirates at sea, then succeeded in capturing Olympus; Zenicetes, despairing of further resistance, set fire to his house and perished with his family in the flames. Servilius thereupon annexed his 'kingdom' to the province of Cilicia. He did not, however, proceed against the main pirate strongholds in Rough Cilicia, but marched inland to deal with the bandits of Isauria. In spite of his successes, therefore, the pirates remained unsuppressed. But not for long. In 67 B.C. Pompey was appointed to an extraordinary command with almost unlimited powers and resources for the complete and final extermination of piracy from the whole Mediterranean. His success was rapid and brilliant. Following a naval victory off Coracesium (now Alânya), he besieged the pirates in their fortresses on land, and by granting generous terms to those who surrendered brought his campaign to a completely satisfactory conclusion in a matter of weeks. Rough Cilicia was now added to the province, whose name thus ceased for the first time to be a misnomer, and piracy was never again so

[1] Below, p. 124.

serious a nuisance to the Roman power. A year or two later Smooth Cilicia was also incorporated.

But the Roman republic was now entering on a period of civil war which proved to be more than it could survive. Upon the death of Caesar on the Ides of March 44 B.C. his murderers, Brutus and Cassius, found themselves opposed by Octavian and Mark Antony; with the object of raising troops, and more especially money, they toured Asia demanding exorbitant contributions from the provincials; the amount required is said to have been the equivalent of ten years' taxes. Following their defeat at Philippi in 42 B.C. Antony was assigned the command of the east; with no one to oppose him he quickly assumed virtually monarchical powers, adopting the title of 'latter-day Dionysus'. He repeated the requisitions of money made by the tyrannicides, and among his many high-handed actions was the presentation of the great library of Pergamum to Cleopatra—that is, he added it to the even greater library at Alexandria. The eastern parts of Asia Minor, which were not yet incorporated as provinces in the Roman dominions, Antony presented to various local rulers, known as client kings; one of these, Amyntas of Galatia, received, together with other regions, at least a part of Pamphylia, where he struck coins at Side (36 B.C.).

Antony's reign was brought to an end at the sea-battle of Actium in 31 B.C., where he and Cleopatra were crushingly defeated by Octavian. This was the finish of the Roman republic. Under the victor, who now assumed the title of Augustus, the empire was established (27 B.C.).

To the eastern provincials the change brought nothing but good. Superficially no doubt things continued much as under the republic: every year the province received its governor, the tax-gatherers functioned as before, and the Italian bankers and merchants continued to grow rich. But provincial governors were now appointed, in most cases, by the emperor himself, and were responsible to him, and in general it was much easier to secure satisfaction for their misconduct. And for three hundred years the south and west of Asia Minor were free from warfare. The Roman imperial policy, apart from financial matters, was to leave the cities to manage their own affairs and to develop their economy in peace. Those which had been given their freedom under the republic continued for the most part to enjoy it; such cities were, in theory at least, exempt from taxation and were not subject to the governor's orders. In Pamphylia, Aspendus, Perge, Sillyum and Side appear to have possessed this status; at all events they were permitted to issue their own autonomous coinage.

Soon after the establishment of the empire, in 25 B.C., Amyntas died and his kingdom of Galatia was converted into the Roman province of that name. What was done with Pamphylia at this time is not known with certainty; some scholars have thought it was included in the new province, others, with perhaps less probability, that it was made into a province of Pamphylia by itself.

The year A.D. 43 saw the final and permanent disposition of the country. In that year it was joined by Claudius with Lycia, which had hitherto been free and independent, in the new province of Lycia-Pamphylia. These oddly assorted territories, so utterly unlike in the nature of the country and in the character of the inhabitants, continued till the fourth century to be administered officially as a single unit under a single governor; but in other respects each maintained its own individuality. So the cities of each united in a separate commonalty, with its own council and magistrates, which conducted its affairs independently of the other. The inclusion of Lycia completed the incorporation in the empire of the whole of Asia Minor.

These provincial commonalties also conducted all kinds of relations with Rome. Among these must be counted the worship of the emperor. The elevation of human beings to divinity was familiar from the time of the heroes: Asclepius and Heracles are examples: and in Hellenistic times the deification and worship of the kings in their lifetime had been the normal practice. The eastern provincials accordingly desired to treat the emperor in the same fashion, but to the Romans the idea was distasteful; Augustus and his successor Tiberius were unwilling to be worshipped as gods. But a beginning had already been made under the republic with the institution in a number of cities in Asia of a cult of the deified Rome, and Augustus

reluctantly agreed to the addition of his own name to this.
Later emperors were less bashful and more ready with their
permission; by the second century A.D. most cities possessed
one or more temples devoted to the imperial cult. Pamphylia
was not behindhand; the inscriptions of Attaleia, Perge,
Sillyum and Side make frequent mention of priests or high-
priests of the cults of Rome and of the emperors.

These temples were erected by permission of the Roman
Senate or of the emperor himself, and each carried with it the
city's right to style itself Neocorus, 'Temple-Warden'; Side
boasted itself 'Six times Temple-Warden'.[1] In the absence of any
form of warfare during the long *pax Romana*, titles and honours
of this kind were all that the cities had to strive for. They were
highly prized and proudly set forth on the city's coins and
inscriptions: Free, Autonomous, Friend and Ally of Rome,
Metropolis of Pamphylia and many more.

Another function of the provincial commonalties was the
celebration every four years of a great festival including
athletic, dramatic and other competitions. Athletics had been
popular in Greek lands since Homeric times. The games at
Olympia were begun according to tradition in 776 B.C., and
those at Delphi, Nemea and the Isthmus were instituted in the
sixth century. During the classical and Hellenistic periods
many other cities followed this example, and by the time of the
Roman empire the athletic festivals celebrated in all parts of
the world (not least in Asia) were counted by the hundred.
Sport had by then long since become professionalised, and
every summer crowds of pot-hunters made their way from
city to city in search of the money-prizes which were now
commonly given, and of the honours and rewards which a
successful athlete might expect in his own home town. In
addition to these local celebrations it became the custom for
each province to hold games in its own name; these would take
place in the larger cities of the province in turn, and normally
carried more prestige than the festivities of the individual
towns.

As was said above, it was in general the Roman policy to

---

[1] This does not necessarily mean that Side possessed six temples
dedicated to the imperial cult; see below, p. 97.

interfere as little as possible in the affairs of the various cities. Supreme authority was, of course, in the hands of the provincial governor, but for the most part the cities were left to manage their own daily concerns. As in the old days of independence the council and people held their separate assemblies for this purpose, though now, of course, with greatly restricted powers; in fact, the activity of which we hear most in the inscriptions is their bestowal of honours, coupled generally with the erection of a statue, upon Roman officials in gratitude for their good government and upon citizens or others who had served the city well. During the time of prosperity under the early empire, when wealth was abundant, the richer citizens were eager to outdo one another in making lavish presentations to their home town; handsome buildings were erected at private expense, while other benefactors undertook out of their own pockets to organise an athletic festival, to supply oil in the gymnasium free of charge, or simply to make a distribution of money either to all the citizens or to certain sections of them. These and many other benefactions we find recorded on the bases which are usually all that remain of the statues with which these men were honoured.

In the second century, under the 'good emperors' from Trajan to Marcus Aurelius, the standard of living in the province as a whole was higher than it has ever been since. The third century, on the other hand, brought a definite deterioration. Of the many emperors, some of them barbarians, who ruled uneasily for short periods before meeting with some form of violent death, a few were good and capable rulers; but the incapacity of the majority for controlling an empire, and the lack of continuity in the government, led to a serious weakening of the Roman authority in the provinces. Taking advantage of this, the inhabitants of the highlands to the north of Pamphylia attempted to push south to the richer coastal regions; for the most part they were repulsed by the Roman troops, but they did much damage, and in general the third and fourth centuries were bad times for the province.

Christianity does not appear to have taken a very early hold in Pamphylia. St. Paul passed through Perge on his way to Pisidian Antioch, and he preached there on his return journey; but he does not seem to have stayed there long, and we do not hear of the foundation of any church in that region, nor is any of his extant letters addressed to any Pamphylian city. By the end of the third century, however, we find a considerable Christian community in the province, and towards A.D. 400 a synod of twenty-five Pamphylian and Lycaonian bishops assembled at Side to devise measures against the troublesome sect of the Euchites. Jews there must always have been, at least in the commercial ports of Side and Attaleia; at Side two separate synagogues are attested by inscriptions.

The reforms carried out by the Emperor Diocletian (284–305), and continued by his successors, included an extensive reorganisation of the provinces, by which many of the larger were split up into two or more parts, and boundaries were readjusted. In the course of these changes the uneasy union of Lycia and Pamphylia was at last dissolved, and each became a separate province. The later history of the country under the Byzantine empire, the Arab invasions, the Crusades and the Turkish conquest, lie beyond the range of the present work.[1]

[1] As was said above, I have made a slight exception in the case of Alânya (chapter 7).

PART TWO

Pamphylia

*

CHAPTER TWO

Attaleia (Antalya)

TRAVELLING SOUTHWARD from Burdur to the sea, the motorist descends in a series of steps. After crossing the flat plain of Bucak he drops into the pass called Çubuk Boğazı and emerges into the plain of Pamphylia near the old Seljuk caravanserai known as Kırkgöz Hanı. Some seven miles from Antalya this plain is divided by a low step into two levels, and the last step of all is formed by the cliffs of Antalya itself. Here for the last two thousand years has been the principal south-coast port; but, as usually happens when a site has been continuously inhabited since antiquity, nothing remains of the original city, and very little of the Roman buildings which later adorned it. The town is nevertheless very attractive, with its picturesque little harbour at the foot of the cliffs, the narrow streets and houses in the old part inside the walls, the numerous Seljuk and Ottoman monuments which survive more or less intact, and not least the mountains of Lycia across the bay.

Attaleia was founded by, and named after, Attalus II, king of Pergamum, in the second century B.C.; the circumstances were recorded above. Whether there was any earlier habitation on the spot is not known; in any case it is certain that this is not, as Beaufort imagined, the site of Olbia.[1] Before long Attaleia replaced Side as the chief port of Pamphylia, but in spite of this pre-eminence it has little history. Pompey used the city as a base during his campaign against the pirates; St. Paul passed through on his return from Pisidia; and in A.D. 130 Hadrian visited Attaleia in the course of a tour of the empire. This last occasion the Attaleians celebrated by restoring and embellishing their city, among other things with

---

[1] For Olbia see below, pp. 109–12.

the fine triple gate which is still standing. It is probable that the Emperor Lucius Verus also called there in A.D. 162 on his way to the Parthian War. At some comparatively late date the city was given the status of a Roman colony. As a bishopric Attaleia was at first under the metropolitan of Perge-cum-Sillyum, but in 1084 was itself raised to the rank of metropolis by the Emperor Alexius I Comnenus.

The city was from the first encircled by a fortification-wall; the original Hellenistic structure was much altered in Roman times, and early in the tenth century was reinforced by a second wall; an inscription recording this is in the Antalya museum. Under Turkish occupation it was further altered and repaired, and much of it has now totally disappeared. Pre-Turkish work is best seen in a number of the towers and especially in Hadrian's Gate.

Of the towers the most notable are that which is now used as a Clock Tower in the city centre, those on either side of Hadrian's Gate, and the well-preserved Hıdırlık Kulesi at the southern extremity of the wall. This last is reached by entering the park and at once turning right to the cliff-edge. It stands 45 feet high in two storeys, the lower square, the upper round, and was built in or about the second century A.D. It is quite unlike the other towers in the wall, and its purpose is uncertain; a lighthouse has been suggested with some probability, and a mausoleum with much less.

Hadrian's Gate (Hadrianus Kapısı), built in honour of the emperor's visit in A.D. 130, is a handsome three-arched gateway of the familiar Roman type; fragments were found of its dedicatory inscription. Gates of this kind inevitably constitute a weakness from the point of view of defence; but under the *pax Romana* defence was no longer a consideration. The three arches are all of equal size, and their vaults were decorated with square panels containing rosettes; on each face stood four Corinthian columns, one in front of each pier of the gate. The building has recently been extensively restored, and now gives a very good idea of its original appearance (Pl. 2).

Well deserving of a visit is the group of Seljuk buildings which at present includes the museum. It is reached by descending the road which runs steeply down beside the

Clock Tower and immediately turning right. The position is marked by the tall Fluted Minaret (Yivli Minare), which is conspicuous from many parts of the town. This was built by Sultan Alâ-üd-din Keykûbad, founder of Alânya, in the early thirteenth century; the mosque to which it was attached was soon destroyed and replaced by the present building, with six cupolas, which now serves as the museum. At a higher level,

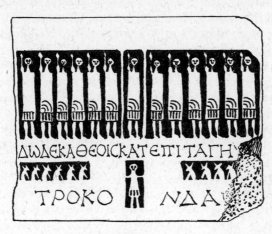

FIG. 2 Antalya museum. Dedication to the Twelve Gods of Lycia

FIG. 3 Terracotta Head in the Antalya museum

close beside the main street, is an attractive *türbe* with a pyramidal roof.

The museum itself, with its surrounding gardens, contains a wide variety of antiquities from numerous sites within the vilâyet of Antalya. Mention may be made of the series of quaint reliefs of the Twelve Gods from Lycia, a collection of tombstones from Aspendus, a remarkable archaic terracotta head thought to be of Cyprian workmanship, a group of handsomely decorated sarcophagi from Perge, and a casket containing bones supposed to be those of St. Nicholas of Myra, better known as Santa Claus.

Many other Seljuk and Ottoman mosques stand in various parts of the town. Among the most interesting is that known as the Kesik Minare, originally a basilica dating to about the fifth century A.D. and later converted to a mosque. It is now reduced to a sad state of ruin.

★

CHAPTER THREE

Perge

AS A GENERAL RULE the early settlers in Asia chose for preference as a site for their city either a narrow-necked peninsula or a hill of moderate height close to the sea; but from Antalya eastwards the Pamphylian coast offers no site of either of these types. Most of the early cities accordingly were founded some distance from the shore, where suitable flat-topped hills were available. Perge, Aspendus and Sillyum are all of this type, and until the founding of Attaleia Side was the only port on the coast of Pamphylia.

Strabo says that Perge may be reached by sailing sixty stades (about seven miles) up the river Cestrus, now the Aksu. Seven miles is, in fact, the distance of Perge from the sea, but the Aksu nowhere approaches within three miles of the city. We may probably infer from Strabo that Perge had a scala on the river at the nearest point to the city.

That Perge was founded by the 'mixed multitude' of Greek immigrants after the Trojan War may be taken as certain. That this was at least the belief of its later inhabitants is proved by the interesting series of statue-bases of 'founders' recently excavated at the main gate.[1] These include both Calchas and Mopsus, the traditional leaders of the migration. It is also certain that the original settlement was on the hill immediately above the existing ruins; but of the city's early history nothing is known. Its first appearance in the records (apart from a mention by the mid-fourth-century geographer, the pseudo-Scylax) is with the arrival of Alexander in 333 B.C. Habitation had by then undoubtedly spread to the level ground below the acropolis hill; since neither the upper nor the lower town was at that time walled, the Pergaeans offered no

[1] Below, pp. 52–3.

resistance to the Macedonian. They seem indeed to have taken his part willingly; at least, Pergaean guides served to lead a portion of his army over the mountains from Phaselis to the north, and Alexander seems to have used Perge as a base during his sojourn in Pamphylia. At some time after Alexander's death, and apparently under the rather uncertain rule of the Seleucid kings of Syria, the lower city was at length fortified. Seleucid power in these parts was broken by the battle of Magnesia in 190 B.C.; nevertheless, when Manlius arrived two years later he found a Seleucid garrison still in occupation of Perge. Indignant at this unexpected presumption, he advanced on the city; whereupon the garrison commander came out to meet him and ask his indulgence, explaining that he was merely holding the city, entrusted to him by Antiochus, till he should be told what to do; so far no instructions whatever had arrived. He therefore begged for a month's delay while he ascertained the king's wishes. Manlius consented, and when some days later Antiochus' answer arrived the commander surrendered the town. It appears from this that the king was guilty merely of an oversight, not of a serious attempt to maintain his hold on Pamphylia.

Little or no trace of Pergamene control in the second century is to be seen at Perge; it was, however, during this period that the city's coinage, begun probably under the Seleucids, became abundant. From the first, and throughout its subsequent history, the dominant type on the coins is the famous Pergaean Artemis, whose cult was not only supreme at Perge but was observed in many other places of the ancient world. On the earliest coins her title, in the Pamphylian dialect and script, is Vanassa Preiia, Pergaean Queen, though she is represented as the Greek Artemis. On the second-century coins appears an Ionic temple containing an effigy in the form of a baetyl—a square block of stone surmounted by a human bust. This is evidently the cult-statue of the goddess, and reveals her nature as an old Anatolian deity, originally no doubt a meteoritic block fallen from heaven, later identified by the Greeks with their own Artemis. This same baetyl appears also, at a later date, on the coins of other cities of Pamphylia and Pisidia, as for example Attaleia, Selge, Isinda,

Pednelissus and Pogla—a remarkable tribute to the fame and authority of the Pergaean goddess. Her temple, as with all the more famous deities of antiquity, grew rich with the offerings of the faithful, and afforded a handsome source of plunder to the notorious Verres in 79 B.C.[1]

A highly valued privilege of many ancient sanctuaries was that of asylum, which conferred inviolability on anyone sheltering within its precincts. So greatly prized indeed was it that in the course of time many temples had appropriated it without justification; and in A.D. 22 the Emperor Tiberius held

FIG. 4 Coin of Perge showing Artemis Pergaea

an investigation into the various cases. Whether Perge made a claim for her Artemis we do not know, but she was not among the accepted; and, in fact, it is not until the middle of the third century that the title 'Inviolable' appears on the coins and inscriptions of the city. Its acquisition was celebrated by instituting a festival under the name of the Asyleia Augusteia.

Pergaean Artemis, like the Ephesian Artemis, never became a wholly Greek goddess, but always retained something of her primitive nature. Under the Roman empire the coins continue to show her in her temple in the form of a block of stone, with even less resemblance than before to the human figure (Fig. 4, Pl. 7). It was no doubt because she was conceived as having originally descended from the skies that she was identified with the Greek moon-goddess Artemis; the star and

[1] Above, p. 32.

crescent moon that appear on many coins of Perge also indicate her celestial character. Her cult was served by both priests and priestesses, the latter not necessarily virgins; and for the festival celebrated every year in her sanctuary female superintendents were regularly appointed.

We learn from the ancient lexicographers that the expression 'an Artemis of Perge' was used to mean an itinerant beggar. The writers who record this curious fact explain it by saying that the goddess was in the habit of wandering about and collecting alms. What lies behind this is doubtful; it may be that certain priests attached to her cult were accustomed, like certain friars of more recent times, to act in this way; or we may explain the goddess's wandering, if not her begging, by her lunar character; the moon, in contrast to the fixed stars, was always thought of as a wanderer.

Some fifty years ago there was found an inscription containing part of an inventory of the treasures in the temple of Artemis; it mentions with remarkable frequency solar discs given as offerings. Furthermore, certain coins of Perge, inscribed as usual with the name of Artemis, show her head and that of Apollo together on the obverse. The reverse has Artemis alone. From this it has been inferred that the cult of the moon-goddess was associated in the same sanctuary with that of the sun-god Apollo; if so, we have a further example of the preponderance of the female side in the Anatolian pantheon, for at Perge the cult of Apollo was insignificant by comparison with that of his sister.[1]

Despite the Asiatic character of her principal deity the city was thoroughly Greek. Her civic institutions were purely Hellenic, and the personal names occurring in the inscriptions are almost without exception Greek—or, of course, Roman; not more than 1 or 2 per cent are Anatolian. Much the same is true at Side also; not so, however, at Aspendus.

Early in the second century A.D. the city gained much in beauty from the benefactions of a certain rich lady by the name of Plancia Magna; there will be more to say of her below.

[1] This was not always so, however; for example, in the oracular sanctuaries of Didyma and Claros, where Apollo and Artemis had each a cult, the male deity is dominant.

1   Antalya. The Harbour from the south.

2 Antalya. Hadrian's Gate.

[*opposite*]

3 Antalya. Hıdırlık Kulesi.

4 Perge. The Theatre.

9 Perge. Outer and Inner Gates.

10   Perge. The Stadium, City-Walls and Acropolis, from the Theatre.

11   Perge. The Inner Gate.

12   Perge. The Main Colonnaded Street.

13   Sillyum. The Site from Asar Köyü.

16   Sillyum. The Pamphylian Inscription.

[*opposite*]

14   Sillyum. Late Building of unknown purpose.

15   Sillyum. The Southern Ramp.

17   Sillyum. Rock-cut Steps and Houses.

18   Sillyum. Tower in the Lower Fortification.

20 Aspendus. Exterior of the Theatre.

19 Aspendus. Turkish Bridge over the Eurymedon.

21   Aspendus. The Theatre.

22   Aspendus. The Theatre.

23   Aspendus. Stage-Building in the Theatre.

26   Aspendus. The Aqueduct.

[*opposite*]

24   Aspendus. Annexe to the Basilica.

25   Aspendus. Nymphaeum (?).

27   Aspendus. Rock-cut Tomb.

28   Aspendus. The Stadium.

The third century also was a time of prosperity for Perge. In addition to the right of asylum she acquired the title of Neocorus, or Temple-Warden. This was normally given by virtue of the possession of a temple for the worship of the emperor; it is surprising that in a city so distinguished the title should appear so late. About the same time, too, Perge was granted the rank of metropolis, and on her coins calls herself 'First' or 'First in Pamphylia'. It is true that Side also was using the same title at the same time, and the word must be taken in less than its literal sense; there can hardly be two first cities, but there can be two cities of the first class.

Among the few Pergaeans who attained to any distinction the most notable is the Alexandrian mathematician Apollonius, who was among the successors of Euclid in the third century B.C. He was the first to make a study of the properties of ellipses, and the first to conceive the epicyclic system of the universe which was later developed by Ptolemy.[1] Mention may also be made of the philosopher Varus in the third century A.D., who was given the nickname Stork by reason of his red, beak-like nose; we read that portraits of him showing this feature were dedicated in the temple of Artemis at Perge.

Unlike the Aspendians, the Pergaeans seem to have maintained good relations with the men of Side; the coinage of both cities includes alliance coins between the two. Aspendus was apparently less neighbourly; no alliance coins with any city seem to be known.

From the main highway a side-road turns off at Karanlık Sokak towards the ruins of Perge; it brings the visitor first to the theatre. This is a moderately well preserved specimen of the Graeco-Roman type; that is to say, a Greek theatre later converted to the Roman style. Its appearance has been much improved recently by clearing out from the orchestra a great part of the mass of fallen blocks which formerly encumbered it; the decoration of the stage has also been partially uncovered, and proves to be in reasonably good condition. As at Side, there was a frieze of panels representing mythological scenes (Pl. 5, 6, 8); unfortunately these have suffered some

[1] Appendix II.

damage in the process of clearing. The stage-building was in several storeys and still stands (in places very precariously) to a considerable height; in the bottom storey a handsome vaulted hall is well preserved.

The cavea is more than a semicircle, in the Greek style, and is separated from the stage-building by the passages called parodoi; these were blocked by fallen débris, but a way has

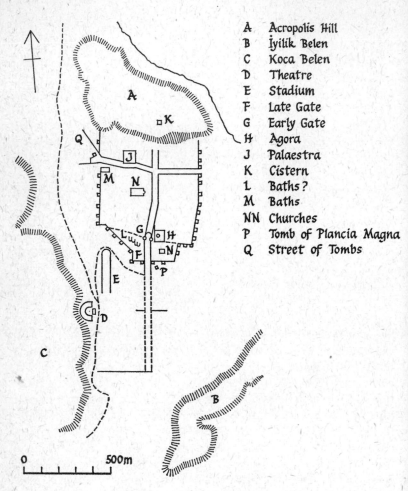

A	Acropolis Hill
B	İyilik Belen
C	Koca Belen
D	Theatre
E	Stadium
F	Late Gate
G	Early Gate
H	Agora
J	Palaestra
K	Cistern
L	Baths?
M	Baths
NN	Churches
P	Tomb of Plancia Magna
Q	Street of Tombs

FIG. 5 Plan of Perge

now been cleared on the south side for the entrance of visitors. The seating space is divided horizontally by the usual diazoma (Pl. 4), and vertically by thirteen stairways below the diazoma, twice as many above it. Allowing 16 inches per person,[1] some 14,000 spectators could be accommodated, though perhaps not in the greatest comfort. Round the top of the cavea runs an arcaded gallery, a normal feature in the Roman period; at its middle point is an entrance from the hillside at the back. On either side, at the level of the diazoma, two large vaulted passages, called vomitoria, also afforded entrance from the hillside. In addition the parodoi, too, were used for entrance and exit, so that in this respect the theatre at Perge is better equipped than that of Aspendus.

At some later date the outer face of the theatre was converted into a nymphaeum by the erection of a great wall, 40 feet high, backing against the stage-building. In its façade are five large niches; these contained water-basins serving as public fountains, but of the actual installations little or nothing is now to be made out.

Between the theatre and the walled city lies the stadium (Pl. 10), one of the best preserved in Asia Minor; the arena, with its surrounding banks of seats, is complete. The northern end is rounded; the southern is at present open, for the ornamental entrance which once stood here has disappeared, nor is there any surviving trace of the starting-gate for the foot-races. The seating capacity is about the same as that of the theatre. Under the seats along the east side is a row of thirty chambers opening to the east; at the back of every third one is a door leading through to an open passage which ran round the arena at ground-level, but was separated from it by a barrier no longer standing. On the other side of the passage is a wall, 6 feet high, below the bottom row of seats; the doors seem therefore to lead neither to the arena nor to the seats, and we must apparently suppose that wooden steps were installed for spectators' use. There is also an outer staircase at the north end of the stadium. The other twenty chambers were used as shops; in some of them is written on the wall the name of the owner or, in one or two cases, of his trade.

[1] See below, p. 129, n.1.

The main part of the city is surrounded, as was said above, by a wall dating from the third century B.C. Especially on the east side this wall is in good preservation, and a number of its towers are still standing almost to their full height; it contains three principal gates, on the west, east and south, and several posterns. There are, in fact, two south gates, for at a late date —hardly earlier than the fourth century A.D.—a long stretch of the wall on the south side was dismantled and a new wall

ΚΤΙΣΤΗΣ
ΚΑΛΧΑΣ ΘΕΣΤΟΡΟΣ
ΑΡΓΕΙΟΣ

FIG. 6 Perge. The 'Founder' Calchas

built to enclose a larger area, with a new gate (F) about 80 yards to the south of the old gate. The masonry of this later wall is much inferior to the earlier (Pl. 9).

The older gate G is at present the most interesting part of the city. Its general form is that of a horseshoe-shaped court flanked by two towers, a type which we shall see repeated at Sillyum and Side. The towers at Perge, unlike the others, are round and are still standing to most of their height (Pl. 11). At the inner end of the horseshoe a triple-arched gateway was erected; this is a Roman feature and did not form part of the original layout. Only the lowest portions of it remain. In the walls of the court are niches which once held statues, and on a

ledge at the foot of the wall stood other statues. The bases of
these latter have survived with their inscriptions, which
designate the statues as those of the founders of the city. Nine
of these have been recovered during the excavation conducted
by the Archaeological Department of Istanbul University in
1954–6; it is probable that there were five on each side and
that one is lost. The 'founders' include heroes of the mythological age, some, such as Mopsus and Calchas, familiar (Fig.
6), others obscure or quite unknown. No doubt all of these
were supposed by local tradition to have come with the
settlers after the Trojan War. But two of the bases—the first
and third from the south on the east side—bear the names of
M. Plancius Varus and his son, C. Plancius Varus. The
inclusion of these Romans with the heroes of the distant past
is due to the use of the word 'founder' in late times to describe
anyone who had paid from his own pocket for the construction
of buildings in the city; by an amiable exaggeration he is
regarded as a sort of second founder. What buildings Varus
and his son paid for we do not know. The inscriptions call
them, rather surprisingly at first sight, father and brother of
Plancia Magna; relationships are not normally defined by
reference to the distaff side. Surprise is, however, reduced by
the great number of other inscriptions mentioning this lady.
In and around the south gate, and elsewhere in the city, at
least fourteen other texts have been found recording either
dedications of statues made by her or statues of her decreed by
the city authorities. Those presented by her are all of members
of the Roman imperial house and were erected about A.D. 120.
Plancia herself was priestess of Artemis and of the Mother of
the Gods, and held the highest civic office of state, that of
demiurgus. It was not unusual in Roman times for a woman to
hold public office, though in many cases her service would in
practice be confined to the disbursement of the necessary
money.

M. Plancius Varus is known from other sources. He had a
distinguished political career at Rome, was consul in or about
A.D. 71 and proconsul of Asia some eight years later. On their
statue-bases at the south gate he and his son are called
Pergaeans; this need not necessarily mean that Perge was their

home town, for honorary citizenship was very often conferred
on distinguished men from other cities, but there is no
particular reason to suppose that this was done in Varus' case.
At least it is clear that his family was settled at Perge in the
early second century.

Internally the city is divided into four quarters by two
colonnaded streets which cross at right-angles towards the
north end of the city. They are not quite straight, and are
presumably an addition to the original layout, having to
diverge slightly to avoid existing buildings which could not be
scrapped. Down the middle of each ran a water-channel, a
familiar feature in ancient cities which may be seen repeated
in Antalya today (Pl. 12). The channels are barred at intervals
of 25 feet by cross-walls whose purpose was partly to check the
flow of the water and partly to facilitate cleaning. The water
was brought from the high ground on the west to the west gate
and from there to the south gate, beyond which the street
continued for nearly half a mile outside the city. On either side
of the street was a colonnaded portico, or stoa, and behind
this a row of shops; the same arrangement may be seen at Side,
and was indeed usual. Outside the city little trace of the street
remains visible, but the canal at its southern end presents a
curious appearance that attracted the attention of Charles
Fellows in 1838. The lime with which the water is impregnated
has gradually built up a deposit which has completely covered
the masonry of the canal so as to give it the appearance of a
solid stone wall. Though it puzzled Fellows, this phenomenon
is not, in fact, particularly rare; the same thing may be
observed, for example, at Evdir Hanı[1] and at Hierapolis in
Lydia.

Lying in the main street the visitor may notice the recently
excavated block illustrated in the adjoining sketch (Fig. 7).
It is evidently a gaming-board, but what game was played on
it is unknown. Not, certainly, the game of *pessoi* of which we
read in the ancient texts from Homeric to Roman times, and
which seems to have been a kind of draughts or chess; we have
not much information about this game, but we do know that
the men were arranged in five lines, and that only as a last

[1] Below, p. 112.

resource was a man moved off the back line. Our board, where
the squares are set in longitudinal lines of six, is obviously
quite unsuitable for this. It would no doubt be easy enough
to devise some appropriate rules; at all events, whatever game
was played on it was evidently very popular, as stones
similarly marked out are frequently found in various parts of
Asia Minor.

FIG. 7 Perge. Gaming table

Just beside the early south gate G, on the east, is a large
square space surrounded, like the main street, by a stoa with
chambers behind. These, too, appear to be shops, and the
whole is evidently a market-place, or agora. In the middle of
the square is a round building, adding one more to the
numerous resemblances between Perge and Side. This agora
overlaps the line of the original south wall of the city, and
must obviously have been constructed after that was levelled,
that is after the enlargement of the city in the fourth century.
There must have been an earlier agora, but it has not been
located.

Another building which belongs to the later enlarged city is
that whose massive ruins (L) stand close to the south gate on
the west of the street. This is thought to be a baths, though the
arrangement of its rooms is hardly normal, nor is there any
obvious provision for a supply of water. A much more normal

baths is that which exists close to the west gate (M on the plan); the date of this has not been established.

The building J, on the other hand, is quite closely dated by its inscription; it was dedicated to the Emperor Claudius (A.D. 41–54) by a certain C. Julius Cornutus. It comprises a large open square and is identified as a palaestra. Its south wall, with numerous windows overlooking the street, is comparatively well preserved. A palaestra normally formed part of a gymnasium, and its sides were flanked by rooms serving both for those who used the gymnasium for athletic exercise and as schoolrooms; excavation will be needed before these can be identified. This is the earliest datable building at Perge apart from the city walls.

In late Roman or early Byzantine times the walled city seems to have been abandoned, and the population withdrew to the acropolis hill where the original Perge was founded. This contraction of the city again finds its parallel at Side. The scanty remains on the flat surface of the hill seem all to belong to this late period. No fortification walls of any period exist on the hill; they were evidently considered, with good reason, to be unnecessary. There was, however, some kind of gateway at the top of the only slope, on the south side, by which the hill can be ascended, but it is now completely destroyed. Close to this point, at K, is a large rectangular cistern, some 45 feet square, with vaults supported on short pillars largely formed of reused materials. This cistern was mistaken by earlier travellers for a church.

The tombs at Perge were placed, in the usual ancient fashion, beside the roads leading to the city gates. That on the north-west (Q on the plan) was excavated in 1946 by the Turkish Historical Society, and a handsome street of tombs was brought to light. More than thirty sarcophagi were unearthed, most of them sculptured and inscribed. The condition of this street has deteriorated in the last twenty years, but a number of the more important tombs may be seen in the Antalya museum. Just outside the later city gate, at P, are the scanty remains of a once impressive tomb, identified by fragments of its inscription as that of the rich benefactress Plancia Magna.

The outstanding mystery at Perge concerns the whereabouts of the famous temple of Artemis, of which hitherto no trace has been found. Two passages in the ancient authors afford a general indication. Strabo, writing in the time of Augustus, says it was close to the city on high ground; the orator Polemo, in the time of Hadrian, says it was outside the city and calls it 'a marvel of size, beauty and workmanship'. It was therefore, as we should expect, a large temple; it is true that the coins of Perge show it with only two columns on the front, but this was undoubtedly done simply in order to show the cult-image and other objects in the interior unobscured by a row of columns. It is surprising that a large temple on high ground near the city should have disappeared so completely. Had it been on the plain it might easily have become buried, like the temple of Artemis at Ephesus, but on a hill this cannot so readily happen; on a hill-*top* it could hardly happen at all, so that we shall probably be justified in looking for it on a hillside. The blocks might, of course, be carried off for building, but the foundations at least ought to be surviving somewhere.

The first theory put forward by modern scholars was that the temple stood on the acropolis hill, and in particular that its site was marked by the supposed church mentioned above (K). Churches commonly succeeded to the old pagan temples, just as the churches in their turn were often converted into mosques; and the place itself seemed appropriate. But this theory was much weakened when the 'church' was recognised as being in reality a cistern; nor is the acropolis hill naturally described as outside the city; it is rather a part of it. In 1946 a party of Turkish archaeologists sank trenches in all the likely-looking places on the hill, but entirely without result.

A much more attractive suggestion was advanced by the Italian archaeologist B. Pace. The fragmentary temple-inventory mentioned above was found built into a wall near the foot of the hill to the south-east of the city called today Iyilik Belen; such inventories were normally kept in the temple to which they related. And on the slope of this hill are the ruins of a Byzantine church, accompanied by other marks of habitation in late antiquity and two fragments of Greek inscriptions. The Turkish party accordingly turned their

attention to this hopeful-seeming site; but neither under the
church nor on a mound some 200 yards to the north of it,
where there once stood a fair-sized Byzantine building, were
any traces of the temple to be found. Exploration of the hill
to the west called Koca Belen gave equally negative results.
The mystery therefore remains. Yet Iyilik Belen is by far the
most alluring possibility, and we may perhaps be permitted to
hope that more extensive investigations may some day bring
the temple to light.

*

CHAPTER FOUR

Sillyum

WHEREAS THE OTHER ancient cities of the Pamphylian plain,
lying close to the main road, are attracting more and more
visitors every year, Sillyum stands comparatively aloof,
accessible only by indifferent roads, and is rarely visited. Yet
the ruins are impressive and, to the present writer at least, no
whit less interesting and in some ways more attractive than
those of the better-known places.[1] From the main highway, at
a point about twenty-six kilometres from Antalya, a respectable road leads north to the village of Kocayatak; from here
the way is hard to find, and it is best to take a guide. There is
talk of an improved road, but the villagers are lazy, and instead
of making it themselves are waiting for the government to do
it for them. The present track is easily passable for a jeep, and
even, in the dry season, for a private car. The ruins are
approached by the hamlet of Asar Köyü at the south-west
foot (Pl. 13); Yanköy, which sometimes gives its name to the
site, lies on the far side, and the ordinary visitor has no
occasion to go there.

The flat-topped hill which carries the city is conspicuous
from afar; it is easily visible from Perge (as Strabo notes)
and from most parts of the plain. Its flanks are absolutely
vertical in all parts except at one point on the west; in many
places the edges have fallen away, leaving half a cistern, or in
one place half a temple, at the brink of the precipice. The hill
bears a general resemblance to that of Perge, but is considerably higher; the summit is some 700 feet above the sea.

Apart from the incidents narrated by Arrian in connexion

[1] Let the reader not be deterred by the depressing account in
Hachette's World Guide, whose author can surely never have been to
Sillyum.

with Alexander's campaign,[1] Sillyum has virtually no history. It was presumably founded with the other cities, during the migration after the Trojan War; nothing is actually recorded, but the recent discovery among the ruins of a statue-base bearing the name of Mopsus suggests that here, as at Perge, this hero was regarded as a founder. The earliest mention of the city is by the geographer who passes under the name of Scylax in the middle fourth century B.C., shortly before Alexander; the coins begin in the third century, and give the name in the form Selyviys. Strabo refers to the city as forty stades from the sea, lofty and visible from Perge.[2] 'Scylax' and Arrian give the name as Syllium; the form preferred here is that which the city gives itself on its coins of the Roman imperial age. Strabo mentions a large lake Capria in the neighbourhood; of this nothing now remains, but the marshy ground a little west of Aspendus evidently marks its position.

Ascending the hill from Asar Köyü the visitor comes first to the lower gate A. In plan this resembles the main gates at Perge and Side, though on a smaller scale; it comprises a horseshoe-shaped court with a tower on either side. This gate belongs to the later fortification of the city, when the inhabitants preferred to move their dwellings for convenience down from the hilltop to be nearer their fields; this outer wall extends northwards from the gate to the conspicuous tower D.

Although the slope on the west side of the hill is less precipitous than elsewhere, it is still too steep for a direct ascent. For this reason an elaborate ramp was constructed, leading up to the upper entrance from north and south. The northern ramp, B[2], is preserved for a short stretch near the top, where its stone pavement remains; the southern, B[1], survives in its lower part, and is among the more impressive monuments of Pamphylia (Pl. 15). The roadway, 17 feet wide, leads up with the rock-face on the right, and on the left a wall of handsome masonry up to nine or ten courses high, of Hellenistic date. This wall is supported at intervals by

[1] Above, pp. 27–8.
[2] Strabo's manuscripts do not actually name the city, and forty stades (about four and a half miles) is a considerable underestimate, the true figure being more like ten miles; but there is no doubt that Sillyum is the place referred to.

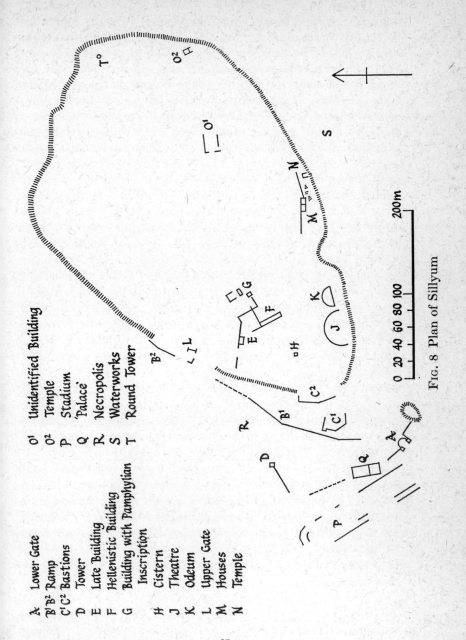

A   Lower Gate
B¹ B²   Ramp
C¹ C²   Bastions
D   Tower
E   Late Building
F   Hellenistic Building
G   Building with Pamphylian
        Inscription
H   Cistern
J   Theatre
K   Odeum
L   Upper Gate
M   Houses
N   Temple

O¹   Unidentified Building
O²   Temple
P   Stadium
Q   'Palace'
R   Necropolis
S   Waterworks
T   Round Tower

0 20 40 60 80 100   200m

Fig. 8 Plan of Sillyum

61

buttresses and contains a series of windows about 6 feet wide
(Pl. 15). It is thought that this ramp, and also the northern,
were probably roofed; the windows are not in themselves
proof of this, but when the ramp was constructed it was outside the city, and a roof would give protection against an
enemy's attack. The two ramps joined at the top and turned
inwards to the city gate L, which is still standing in part.

The centre of the early city lay to the south-east of the
main gate, around the buildings E, F, G. At present the eye is

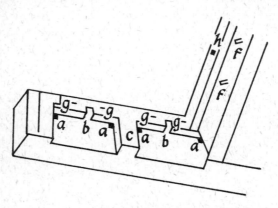

FIG. 9 Sillyum. Holes and slots for fastening window

first taken by a large structure of Byzantine date, standing
almost to its full height (Pl. 14); its purpose is not known. But
more attractive than this are the smaller Hellenistic buildings F
and G. The larger of these, F, was some kind of public hall, and
is well preserved in part. Its west wall is 180 feet long and stands
up to 20 feet high; it contains ten windows, not all of the same
size. The fastenings for one of these (the third from the south
end) are shown in the accompanying sketch. The four holes
a, *a* held uprights to which the four panels of the double fold-
ing windows were attached; the two pairs were divided by a
post which stood on the central projection *c*. The curved slots
f, *f* were evidently for fixing cross-bars to hold the windows
shut. The panels were, of course, of wood, that is shutters, not
glass panes. The other holes *b*, *g* and *h* are not adequately

explained, and the visitor may amuse himself by trying to make sense of them.

G is a much smaller building, with an elegantly decorated door; but it is chiefly remarkable because one of the jambs of the door carries the well-known inscription written in the local dialect and alphabet (Pl. 16). This document is the principal evidence for the Pamphylian language, the other material consisting only of a few short inscriptions and coin-legends. The Sillyum inscription runs to thirty-seven lines (interrupted by a square hole later cut in the jamb), but is very imperfectly understood. The dialect is a form of Greek, and the alphabet is Greek also—that is, it is quite different from the strange language written and spoken at Side, but similar to that of Aspendus and Perge. Individual words and phrases can be made out, including the name Selyviios, but the text as a whole is still obscure. Its date is Hellenistic, probably not far from 200 B.C. By the first century A.D. the dialect had dropped out of use, at least for official purposes, and coins and inscriptions show the normal Greek of the period.

The southern rim of the plateau is full of interest for the visitor. Towards the west end are the two theatres J and K— or, rather, a theatre and an odeum. The theatre J is the larger, but still on the small side; fifteen rows of seats have been counted, with a stairway down the middle. It has at some time been split into two by a huge cleft, where a part of the hill has broken away without falling, leaving a deep chasm some 6 to 10 feet wide; this disaster has destroyed the stage-building except for one corner of the auditorium. The odeum has suffered less; in particular its south wall stands, supported by eight buttresses.

A little to the east is a most attractive group of buildings. The hilltop has been levelled in a series of terraces joined by rock-cut steps; on these terraces stand the remains of private houses whose walls are partly of masonry, partly of the natural rock (Pl. 17). Narrow lanes turn off at intervals to the north. A curious oval hollow in the floor of the westernmost house has not been explained. At N is a small temple 37 by 25 feet, which had originally four columns on its east front; its south wall has fallen down the precipice, but the other walls stand up to eight courses in places. They are of handsome Hellenistic masonry, one narrow course alternating with two broad. Just beyond this is a long underground cistern with gratings in the roadway. All this part of the ruins gives a remarkable feeling of intimacy with the ancient city, such as is not often experienced on totally unexcavated sites.

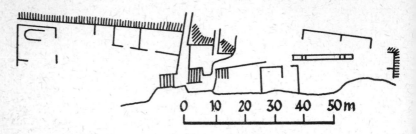

FIG. 10 Sillyum. Houses and steps at the cliff edge

From here it is pleasant to walk round the rim of the plateau, which has a commanding view in all directions. The temple O^2 is badly preserved and has suffered from repairs and rebuilding, nor is the round tower at T of any consequence; but the rock-cut house-foundations and the numerous cisterns all along the north-west edge of the hill are not without interest. And from here the visitor may look down on a part of the ancient necropolis. The tombs are simple rectangular graves sunk into the surface of large masses of fallen rock, with steps leading up; they were closed with separate lids, but none of these now remain. In many cases holes may be seen, intended for the pouring of libations to the dead.

From the upper gate the visitor may descend by the northern ramp B and return to the village by a path passing under the great bastions C^1, C^2 and the southern ramp. On the way he will pass the handsome and well-preserved tower D, standing in the line of the later fortification (Pl. 18). Its outer, or northern, door has a horizontal lintel, the inner door is arched. The tower was in two storeys; from the upper storey doors on east and west opened on to the ramparts, which are not now preserved to so great a height. On north and south are

windows, and on each of the four sides, close to the top, is a
smaller window.

Close below the 'Palace' Q (whose true destination is not
known) is the stadium (P). This is about 195 yards long,
exclusive of the seating. On the west side the seats rested on a
long vaulted gallery not intended for circulation, and on the
east side merely on the sloping ground. The interior of the
stadium is badly ruined.

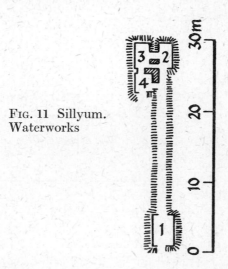

FIG. 11 Sillyum.
Waterworks

One other structure is worthy of a visit by the enterprising
traveller, if he is not of too bulky a build. At the point marked
S on the plan, about half-way up the slope at the foot of the
cliff, is the entrance to a narrow tunnel running some 30 yards
into the hill. Its plan is shown in the adjoining sketch. From
the outer room 1 a passage only about 18 inches wide leads to
the three inner rooms 2, 3 and 4, all of which communicate
with one another. The passage is not comfortable, and a light
is, of course, needed. This interesting installation was at first
thought to be a group of grave-chambers, but it is now agreed
to be a waterworks. The spring is now almost dried up, no
doubt as a result of the seismic shocks which the hill has
suffered, but the strip of green vegetation which is noticeable,
even in the dry season, just below this point shows that

something of it still survives. On a wall of room 1 is a curious inscription praying for the salvation of the ruling emperor.

Besides what has been described above the visitor will notice many other walls and fragments of buildings, for the ruins of Sillyum are very abundant; but until excavation is undertaken their nature is likely to remain unexplained.

★

CHAPTER FIVE

Aspendus

S IDE HAS N O W been largely excavated, and Perge is next in
the queue; Aspendus must wait its turn, but even if that turn
never comes it cannot lose its attraction for the traveller, for
it possesses the finest single monument on the whole coast—its
superb theatre. 'You may have seen amphitheatres in Italy,
France, Dalmatia and Africa; temples in Egypt and Greece;
palaces in Crete; you may be sated with antiquity, or scornful
of it. But you have not seen the theatre of Aspendus.' So D. G.
Hogarth wrote in 1909. The same could hardly be written
today, for these parts are now frequently visited, and the
theatre of Aspendus is familiar to many. There is even a
charge for admission, and an asphalt road leads to the door.
But the building is the same as ever, and the writer well
remembers the feeling, almost of awe, which it gave him when
he first stepped into its interior: 'This is not like anything I
ever saw before.' For those who like their ancient monuments
complete and undamaged (and who does not?) Aspendus is not
to be missed.

Concerning the foundation of the city and its early name
Estwediiys, something was said above.[1] Later Greek tradition
unanimously ascribed the foundation to men of Argos in the
Peloponnese. These were presumably an Argive contingent in
the 'mixed multitude'; on the other hand, their leader Mopsus
is described on his statue-base at Perge as a man of Delphi.
As so often, an 'eponymous' founder was subsequently
invented by the name of Aspendus; he certainly never existed.

By the early fifth century B.C. Aspendus was striking a
silver coinage; of the other Pamphylian cities only Side coined
so soon, and these two were undoubtedly the greatest at that

[1] Above, p. 24.

period. Cimon's double victory over the Persians at the mouth
of the Eurymedon in 469 B.C. was recounted above;[1] it resulted
in Aspendus (and one or two other cities of the south coast)
being incorporated for a time in the Athenian maritime
league (the Delian Confederacy), though we do not know at
what sum in tribute she was assessed, nor that she ever
actually paid.[2] In 449, however, by the terms of the peace
concluded in that year, the Persians recovered control of
Pamphylia; although the Athenians still listed Aspendus as due
for tribute as late as 425, this was only an empty gesture. In
411 the Persians were using the city as a naval base.

In 389 B.C. the Athenian commander Thrasybulus, engaged
in restoring the fortunes of Athens after her disastrous defeat
in the Peloponnesian War, conducted a money-raising cruise
round the coasts of Asia Minor. Arriving at the Eurymedon,
he anchored and succeeded in collecting a contribution from
the Aspendians; his soldiers, however, misbehaved themselves
and damaged the crops, whereupon the inhabitants set on
Thrasybulus and murdered him in his tent.

The arrival of Alexander in 333 B.C. began, here as elsewhere, a new era. The Aspendians' dealings with him, and
subsequently in the Hellenistic period with the Seleucid and
Egyptian kings, with Garsyeris and with Manlius Vulso, have
already been related.[3] Under Roman rule the city continued
to prosper; Strabo calls it 'well populated', and the notorious
governor Verres found it a rich field for looting. In the first
century A.D. it was reckoned the third city of Pamphylia; 400
years earlier it would have been the second. In the third
century it possessed the 'Neocorate', or Temple-Wardenship
of the emperor, which means that it was granted the privilege
of building a temple for his worship. Side, on the other hand,
possessed this privilege six times over. On its coins Aspendus
calls itself 'proud and honoured', 'ally of the Romans'. In the
fifth century the city's name appears as Primupolis, but why

[1] Above, p. 26.
[2] Appendix I.
[3] Above, pp. 27, 29, 30. At the time of Alexander's visit the Aspendians were accused by their neighbours of forcibly occupying land that
did not belong to them. These neighbours were no doubt the men of
Side, whose relations with Aspendus seem normally to have been bad.

this change was made, or how long it lasted, is not known.

Under the empire Aspendus had some importance as a centre of commerce, and among its products was the salt obtained from the neighbouring lake, presumably the Lake Capria mentioned by Strabo;[1] as the lake dried in summer, we are told, the salt was left on its shores, and as often as it was removed it renewed itself overnight. The vine was cultivated in the vicinity, as in so many places, but owing to a false interpretation of the city's name[2] its wine was not permitted to be used for libations to the gods; it was even said that birds would not touch the vine.

Aspendian citizens known to history are very few. In the third century B.C. a certain Andromachus distinguished himself in the army of Ptolemy IV, and after the defeat of the Seleucid monarch Antiochus III at the battle of Rhaphia he was appointed by Ptolemy as governor of Syria and Phoenicia. Later, there was an Aspendian philosopher by the name of Diodorus; his only claim to fame is that, though professedly a Pythagorean, he affected the beatnik habits of the Cynics, with long hair, dirty clothes and bare feet.

Philostratus, in his Life of Apollonius of Tyana, tells a somewhat improbable tale concerning Aspendus. This Apollonius was also a neo-Pythagorean philosopher, living in the time of Augustus and Tiberius; he pretended to supernatural powers, and if all that his biographer tells could be believed, his influence must have been remarkable. Arriving one day in Aspendus he found the city in great distress, for the rich landowners had locked up all the corn with a view to selling it abroad, and the citizens were living on vetch and similar forms of sustenance. Enraged by the chief magistrate's inability to cope with the situation, they set upon him, and Apollonius found him clinging for refuge to the statue of Tiberius. The philosopher was at this time under a five-year vow of silence; but on learning from the magistrate what the matter was, by signs and gestures he calmed the infuriated mob and persuaded them to summon the landowners who were the cause of the trouble. When these (somewhat

[1] Above, p. 60.
[2] A-spendos, 'non-libationary'; but the form is anomalous.

surprisingly) responded to the invitation he was sorely
tempted to break his vow and abuse them roundly; for the
lamentations of the women and children affected him deeply.
Restraining himself, however, he wrote his rebuke on a tablet
and gave it to the magistrate to read aloud. It said: 'The earth
is the mother of all men, but you are guilty of making her your
own mother only; unless you desist I shall not permit you to
live upon her.' Cowed by this threat, the tycoons gave in and
released the corn into the market. The story speaks highly for
Apollonius' reputation for wizardry; one would have expected
them to show more spirit. Philostratus remarks in an interesting parenthesis that the statue of Tiberius was reckoned
more holy than that of Zeus at Olympia, and that a man was
once convicted of impiety because he struck his own slave
while the latter was carrying a silver coin bearing the emper-
or's name and image. That this was not considered ridiculous
shows the strength of the hold that emperor-worship had upon
the eastern provincials.

The majority of visitors will make first for the theatre,
which unquestionably outshines all else at Aspendus. It is, in
fact, the best-preserved Roman theatre, indeed the best-
preserved ancient theatre of any kind, anywhere in the world
(Pl. 20, 21). It was built in the second century A.D., perhaps
under Marcus Aurelius, and was a gift of two brothers, Curtius
Crispinus and Curtius Auspicatus; their dedication of it 'to the
gods of the country and to the Imperial House', in Greek and in
Latin, may still be read over the entrances at either side of the
stage-building.[1] The form of the theatre is characteristically
Roman, and it may be the only theatre that ever stood on this
spot; if there was an earlier structure, it has been completely
overlaid by that now standing. Apart from the actual stage,
which was of wood, and the statues and columns which
adorned its rear wall, the theatre of Aspendus is virtually
intact. One or two damaged places, notably the two end staircases and the arcade which surrounds the cavea at the top,
have been repaired in recent years; opinions will differ as to

---

[1] These inscriptions are now partially concealed by arches subsequently
built in front of them.

whether this is an improvement. When an ancient building is so nearly complete it may be better to leave well enough alone. At present the brilliant white of the new marble is in startling contrast to the old stones, but will, of course, weather in time. The basic material of the building is a rather indifferent pudding-stone; the seats, floors and facings were of marble or near-marble. The vegetation which formerly grew in the cavea has all been removed, for the building is now regularly used for wrestling-matches and other entertainments.

Visitors are at present admitted through the middle door of the stage-building, but this was not an entrance for spectators in antiquity; they entered by the doors at either side already mentioned, and by two smaller doors (now blocked up) opening on the hillside. The stage-building, which still stands to its full height, was long and narrow; it has five doors on the outside, and above these four rows of windows of varying size and shape. Above and below the top row of windows are projecting blocks pierced with holes; these held upright masts from which a great awning was suspended over the spectators. The interior of the stage-building was originally in several storeys, but the horizontal partitions have disappeared.

Entering through the turnstile the visitor finds himself in the orchestra, which is semicircular in the Roman fashion; in front of him rise the forty rows of seats, divided vertically by numerous staircases and horizontally by a single passage, or diazoma (Pl. 22). To left and right are the inner ends of the spectators' entrances, above each of which is a 'royal box'; these boxes were accessible from the stage-building. All round the summit of the cavea runs an arcade; this in its present form is later than the original theatre, and in places has at some time been repaired in brick. At the level of the diazoma a vaulted gallery runs round under the upper seats; it was closed and dark and was intended not for circulation but for constructional purposes only. On a few of the seats are names cut to reserve the places for particular persons; one of these is, rather surprisingly, at the very top. The writer was told that on a recent occasion 40,000 people were crowded into the building; it was constructed to hold barely half that number.

The inner wall of the stage-building, which formed the back

wall of the stage, was very richly decorated, but of this decoration only the parts which were actually let into the wall now survive (Pl. 23). There were originally two ranges of columns, one above the other, and the numerous niches had pediments supported by smaller columns; in the niches stood statues. There are five doors at stage-level and a row of smaller doors below this. Above the upper range of columns is a large triangular pediment, in the middle of which is a figure of Bacchus surrounded by scrolls of flowers. It is popularly supposed by the local Turks that the neighbouring village of Belkis has taken its name from this figure, which they call Bal Kız, the Honey Girl. Belkis, or Balkıs, is the name given in the Koran to the Queen of Sheba.

The stage itself projected some 23 feet from the back wall; it was on the low side, not more than 5 feet 3 inches in height. The small doors at the foot of the back wall were concealed by the stage, which must have had corresponding doors in its own front wall; these would serve for admitting the animals into the orchestra when the theatre was used for wild beast shows. High up in the side walls of the stage are grooves slanting down from the outer edge to the back wall; these are evidence of a sloping wooden roof to the stage, not so much as a protection for the actors but rather to serve as a sounding-board.

A coating of plaster, decorated in places with zigzag painting in red, which now covers part of the stage-wall, is a later addition and indicates that the theatre continued to be used into Byzantine or medieval times.

Many visitors, having seen and enjoyed the theatre, feel that they have done Aspendus and drive away forthwith. This is a pity, for there is much else on the site deserving of attention.

The hill is in general precipitous, about 130 feet high, and was fortified only at the places where gullies afford access; here also were the gates of the city. A deep hollow divides the hill into two very unequal parts; the city-centre was on the larger western part, the smaller eastern part carrying only the theatre. Of the three entrances at A, B and C, the southern at A was the main gate; C is the best preserved, but is now buried to within

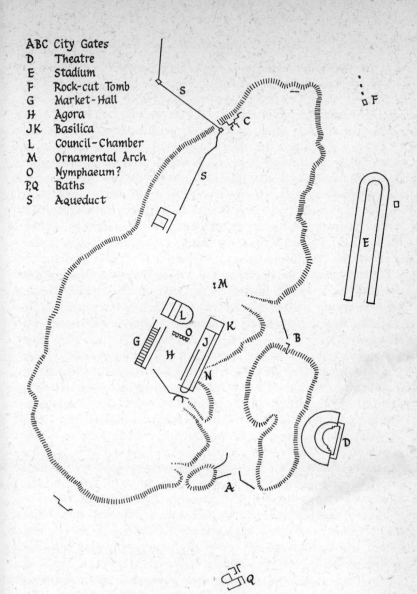

ABC City Gates
D   Theatre
E   Stadium
F   Rock-cut Tomb
G   Market-Hall
H   Agora
JK   Basilica
L   Council-Chamber
M   Ornamental Arch
O   Nymphaeum?
P,Q Baths
S   Aqueduct

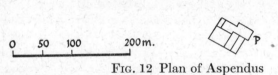

|0   50   100   200 m.|

Fig. 12 Plan of Aspendus

73

two or three feet of the lintel. The wall is seen at its best just to the north of C, where it runs down the hillside in steps and is preserved complete with its coping.

On the level surface of the hill is the agora, or market-place, H, surrounded by the principal public buildings, all of Roman date. On the east side was a great basilica, or hall for the transaction of business, over 100 yards long (J on the plan). Only its foundations remain; towards the south end, at N, they are supported on an arch crossing the gully. At the north end, however, on a higher level, a square building (K on the plan) which formed an annexe to the basilica, still stands to a height of 50 feet, with walls nearly 6 feet thick. It has a single arched door on the north side, and on the south side three doors which led through into the basilica, the middle door much larger than the others. High up in this same wall are two windows, and the west wall is strengthened by four exterior buttresses. The building has at some time been extensively repaired with small stones (Pl. 24).

On the west side of the agora is a long market-hall (G), consisting of a row of shops with a gallery behind and a stoa in front. The shops were in two storeys, as is shown by the holes for the beams carrying the ceilings. None of the columns of the stoa remain, but its position is indicated by the steps about 20 feet from the front of the shops.

The north side of the market-place is occupied by the conspicuous building O, which stands nearly 50 feet high. It consists of no more than a façade, some 40 yards long and only 6 feet thick. The back wall is plain; on the front are two rows, an upper and a lower, of five niches each; the middle niche in the lower row, which is larger than the others, is pierced by a door, and the others have openings now bricked up. Projecting bases at the foot of the wall carried columns, in pairs, supporting an entablature of which parts remain embedded in the wall over the niches. This building is identified as a nymphaeum, that is an installation for distributing water to the city; it would be fed by the aqueduct, which in its surviving part leads in this direction. It is true that the necessary apparatus for a nymphaeum is totally lacking: there are no pipes to be seen, no channels, no water-basins. On the other

hand, the structure bears a striking resemblance to the un-
doubted nymphaeum at Side,[1] and there was found beside it a
dolphin's head with throat pierced to form a water-spout. The
unlikely alternative is that the façade is for decoration only
(Pl. 25).

The purpose of the building L has not been determined. Its
east end is rounded, but there is no trace of any rows of seats;
the suggestion that it was a covered theatre or odeum seems
hardly probable. A council-chamber has also been suggested,
but this is equally uncertain.

At M is a well-preserved single arch, which appears to have
spanned the road leading up from the entrance at B.

But the most striking monument at Aspendus, after the
theatre, is the very fine aqueduct (S), which brought water to
the city from the mountains to the north. It provides probably
the best surviving example of a Roman aqueduct.[2] On descending from the hills to the plain the water was carried on arches
across half a mile of marshy ground to the acropolis; the arcade
served at the same time as a roadway. The greater part of it is
still standing (Pl. 26). An inscription found at Aspendus records
that a certain Tiberius Claudius Italicus presented to the city,
'for the introduction of water', the unusually large sum of two
million denarii—perhaps something like £150,000 at the present
day. That this refers to the construction of the aqueduct is
hardly doubtful; the inscription is apparently of the second
century A.D., and the building may well date to that period.
The water-channel was formed of cubical blocks of stone
pierced through the middle, and was thus capable of with-
standing a very considerable pressure. At the north end, close
to the foot of the mountains, and again about 100 yards from
the acropolis hill, the water was carried up on superimposed
arches to towers some 100 feet high, from which it descended
again on the other side. At the top of each of the towers,
accessible by staircases in the masonry, was an unroofed basin;
the purpose of this was to let the water into the open, thus
allowing the air to escape from the conduit and so reducing the

[1] Below, p. 86.
[2] Others, like the Pont du Garde or the aqueduct at Volubilis, are
rather better preserved, but less interesting in point of construction.

friction which would otherwise impede the flow. The extra
height was necessary in order to avoid loss of pressure on the
far side. It was at one time doubted whether the ancients
understood the principle of piping water up under gravitational

FIG. 13 Tombstone of a priest of Zeus from Aspendus

pressure; if such doubts should remain, the aqueduct at
Aspendus would effectively remove them.

To the north of the theatre is the stadium (E); its state of
preservation is fair, though not so good as at Perge. On either
long side was a vaulted gallery which supported the spectators'
seats; that on the east is preserved up to the spring of the
vault, that on the west is badly ruined. On the outer side of

the eastern gallery is a row of recesses similar to those at
Perge, but smaller; here also they may have served as shops.
In the back wall of most of them is a small window, from which
it may be inferred that the vaulted gallery was used for
circulation, the windows affording a certain amount of light.
Of the starting-line nothing is to be seen.

Close beside the stadium on the east is a built tomb, quite
well preserved, and further to the north is an isolated rock
(F on the plan, Pl. 27) in which has been cut a tomb-chamber
formerly containing a sarcophagus; beyond this on the north
is a row of sarcophagi. To the south of the stadium and a little
east (not shown on the plan) are the ruins of another built
tomb. All these tombs stood evidently beside a road which ran
past the acropolis hill on the east; in the line of this road,
further to the south, when a large drainage trench was opened
in 1947–8, there came to light numerous funeral stelae of the
characteristic Aspendian type. The majority of these are
inscribed merely with the names of the dead man and his
father; some, however, as in the adjoining sketch, are more
decorative. They date for the most part to the Hellenistic
period, and the names are largely Anatolian. Many of them
were taken by the villagers to serve as steps in front of their
houses, where they may still be seen; others are in the Antalya
museum.

The large buildings P and Q are not identified with certainty.
P appears to be a baths, at least from the general layout of its
rooms, though none of the usual apparatus is visible.[1] Q has
been called a baths or a gymnasium; although a second baths
so near the first may seem improbable, this is no doubt the
more likely account; the building has not the normal form of a
gymnasium.

[1] For a typical baths see below, pp. 88–9.

*

CHAPTER SIX

Side

OF THE ANCIENT cities dealt with in the present work Side is the only one which has been systematically excavated. For twenty years, from 1947 to 1966, the work was carried on by the Archaeology Department of Istanbul University under the direction of Professor Arif Müfit Mansel. Excavation and restoration do not always improve the appearance of an ancient site: many people prefer the romantic ruin to the cleared and restored building: but at Side the effect has been wholly to the good. Fellows in 1838 thought the ruins among the least interesting he had seen; he would hardly be of the same opinion today. Shortly before Fellows, in 1812, Captain Beaufort visited the site, and has left us a description which is still useful now; and a little later Daniell went to Side with the fever already upon him from which he died soon after in Antalya. Scientific examination of the ruins began towards the end of the nineteenth century with the party under Count Lanckoronski, who, however, did not excavate; and after the first world war Italian scholars were active in the region. Since 1947 the aspect of the site has changed gradually from year to year; thanks to the Turkish excavations and to the charming situation of the ruins by the sea, Side now attracts numerous visitors all the year round.

A certain air of mystery surrounds the foundation of the city. Strabo and Arrian both say that Side was colonised from Cyme, the Aeolian city on the coast north of Smyrna; and the latter writer adds a curious story, which he says was told by the Sidetans themselves, that immediately upon landing the colonists forgot their Greek and began to speak a barbarian tongue—not, however, that of the neighbouring barbarians, but one peculiar to themselves and hitherto unknown. What lies behind this fairy story is uncertain. So much, however, is beyond doubt, that down to the third century B.C. at least there was spoken and written at Side a language whose words and script are apparently unique. This has long been known from the legends on Sidetan coins, and in recent years three texts in this unknown tongue have been found among the ruins carved on stone, two of them accompanied by a Greek translation. These date to about the third century B.C.; the coins go back to about 500. With this scanty material little progress has been made in deciphering the language, but at the time of writing the newest and longest text has hardly been expertly studied. Two of these stones are now in the museum at Side.

This Sidetan language is quite different from the Pamphylian dialect of Greek which was spoken at Sillyum and Aspendus,[1] and can hardly (despite what Arrian says) be other than the original Anatolian language of Pamphylia. When the colonists from Cyme arrived at Side they must have found this language being spoken; rather surprisingly they seem to have been unable to impose their own Greek in the new city, but were constrained to adopt the local speech. This argues a force of colonists weaker than was usually sent. In fact, we have no evidence of Greek speech at Side before Alexander's conquest of the Persian empire (334–323 B.C.), after which Greek became the official language all over the east, and the local languages gradually died out. At Side we have Greek inscriptions on stone from about 300 B.C. and on coins from the second century onwards.

The Cymaean foundation is likely to date from the seventh or sixth century, at which time many secondary colonies were founded in Asia Minor, but there was certainly earlier habitation on the spot. Eusebius in the fourth century A.D. actually gives 1405 B.C. as the original foundation date, some 200 years before the Trojan War; this information is unlikely to have any sound historical basis, but it does appear that Side was not, like the other Pamphylian cities, founded by the 'mixed multitude' of wandering Greeks after the fall of Troy. The exact nature of the settlement that the Cymaeans found existing must remain uncertain. It is probable that the Greek

[1] Above, p. 24.

Sidetans were ashamed of their barbaric language when the other Pamphylian cities were speaking a form of Greek, and invented the curious story told by Arrian to cover the indignity.

The name Side means 'pomegranate', a familiar symbol of fertility, and this fruit is represented on the city's coins from the earliest down to Roman imperial times (Fig. 14). Though

FIG. 14 Coin of Side
showing pomegranate

used in Greek literature, *side* is not the ordinary Greek for a pomegranate, and is no doubt an early Anatolian word. The same root, and even the same name, recurs in numerous places in Asia. Here again, however, the Greek fondness for an 'eponymous' derivation led to the tradition that the city had its name from a certain Side, daughter of Taurus and wife of Cimolus; this lady unquestionably never existed.

In early times, under the Lydians and then under the Persians, Side has virtually no recorded history apart from that of Pamphylia as a whole. The citizens' reputation was perhaps not of the best, if there is any significance in a story told of the well-known harpist Stratonicus, whose quips were famous. When asked who were the most rascally of mankind, he is said to have replied, 'In Pamphylia the men of Phaselis, in the whole world the men of Side.'[1]

The city's quiet submission to Alexander was mentioned above, as also was her refusal to aid Achaeus against Antiochus III, 'mainly from enmity towards the Aspendians'.[2] A little

[1] Stratonicus evidently reckoned Phaselis in Pamphylia and Side in Cilicia. They are normally assigned to Lycia and Pamphylia respectively. But the boundaries between these regions were ill defined and changeable.

[2] Above, pp. 29–30.

later, in 190 B.C., Side was the scene of a naval battle
between Antiochus' fleet, commanded by Rome's old enemy
Hannibal, and that of the Rhodians, who were fighting in the
Romans' cause. The Sidetans were no doubt supporting the
king, but we hear nothing of them in Livy's account of
the fight. The battle ended in an indecisive victory for the
Rhodians.

During the greater part of the second century Side seems to
have enjoyed the freedom which she had purchased from
Manlius,[1] and never came under the dominion of Pergamum.
It has even been suggested that the figure of Nike, goddess of
victory, which appears on the handsome and abundant
second-century coins of Side may commemorate a victory
won by the city against the Pergamenes; but we have no actual
proof of this.[2]

In the course of this same century the Sidetans became
deeply implicated in the piracy which was then assuming such
formidable proportions. We learn from Strabo that the Cilician
pirates used the harbour of Side as a dockyard, and by agreement with the citizens auctioned their prisoners in the city.
The historian leaves no doubt that the Sidetans were willing
accomplices in this trade, and no doubt made a gratifying
profit from it. When, however, in 67 B.C., Pompey cleared the
pirates from the sea, the citizens hastened to restore their good
name by erecting a handsome monument and statue in his
honour.[3] So far as we know, they suffered no punishment at the
hands of the Roman Senate.

Under the empire Side flourished and grew rich, like most
of the cities of the east, without playing any special part in
history. The decay of the Roman authority in the third
century led to a recrudescence of piracy, and Side suffered
attack and siege by Scythian buccaneers from the Black Sea;
she resisted, however, vigorously and successfully. The inroads
into Pamphylia made in the third and fourth centuries by the
Isaurians of the mountainous country to the north, combined

---

[1] Above, p. 30.

[2] This suggestion has however recently received some support from
finds made at the south-east gate of the city; see below, p. 85.

[3] It should be said that this depends upon the correctness of the present
writer's interpretation of a fragmentary inscription recently found at Side.

with the general decline of Roman power, resulted in an impoverishment of the country; very clear traces of this may be seen at Side. About the middle of the fourth century the inhabited area of the city was reduced by half with the erection of a second, inner city-wall across the waist of the peninsula by the theatre; the whole of the city to the north and east of this was left deserted. Further evidence appears in the statue-bases of Roman emperors which originally stood along the main colonnaded street; those of Diocletian (285–305), Julian (361-3), and Gratian (367–83) have been found during the excavations, and in every case an earlier statue-base has been reused for the purpose. Even for a statue of the emperor the city was evidently too poor to afford a new stone.

Better times came in the fifth and sixth centuries. The city was once again inhabited up to and even beyond its original limits; the buildings, notably the theatre, were repaired, and a Forum of Arcadius (395–408) was built just outside the main gate. In early Byzantine times the metropolitan of Side was reckoned tenth (though later reduced to thirteenth) of all those under the patriarchate of Constantinople, and had fifteen bishoprics under him. But with the Arab invasions in the seventh century the ultimate decline of the city set in. By the end of the tenth century it appears to have been deserted as a result of a conflagration and its population transferred to Antalya; from this circumstance it derives its popular name of Old Antalya. The present village, officially called Selimiye, dates only from the beginning of the present century, when it was founded by a group of Moslem exiles from Crete. Since the city was abandoned the ruins have been increasingly covered by drifts of sand blown in by the southerly winds, and a considerable area in the south-east corner is now deeply buried. It is likely that somewhere under this sand, inside or outside the city-wall, lies the stadium which Side certainly possessed, but of which no trace has yet been found.

The road leading from the south-coast highway brings the visitor, now as in ancient times, to the main gate of the city. Side, lying as it does on almost flat ground, had need of strong fortifications, and the city-wall (A) is, in fact, a fine specimen of an ancient defence work. Across the peninsula it is well preserved,

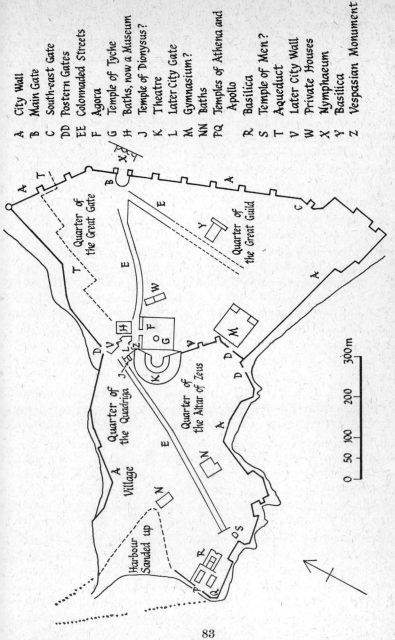

A City Wall
B Main Gate
C South-east Gate
DD Postern Gates
EE Colonnaded Streets
F Agora
G Temple of Tyche
H Baths, now a Museum
J Temple of Dionysus?
K Theatre
L Later City Gate
M Gymnasium?
NN Baths
PQ Temples of Athena and
   Apollo
R Basilica
S Temple of Men?
T Aqueduct
V Later City Wall
W Private Houses
X Nymphaeum
Y Basilica
Z Vespasian Monument

Fig. 15 Plan of Side

Quarter of
the Great Gate

Quarter of
the Great Guild

Quarter of
the Quadriga

Quarter of
the Altar of Zeus

Village

Harbour
Sanded up

0 50 100   200   300m

83

almost to its full height, though at its southern end largely buried under the sand. It is best seen in the neighbourhood of the main gate. The outer face is of regular ashlar, and is adorned, somewhat unusually, by a purely decorative cornice-moulding. The inner side is constructed in three storeys, each projecting beyond the one above, so as to form two passages for the defenders. The topmost storey, which is only partly preserved, consisted simply of a parapet with windows; the middle storey, on the other hand, contained a series of small rooms or casemates with embrasures in the walls. From each of these two storeys, accordingly, fire could be directed upon the enemy. The lowest storey served merely to support the upper parts; it is in some places a plain wall, in others it is equipped with pillars or arches. The wall is further strengthened by towers at unequal intervals; surprisingly, the curtain walls are interrupted behind each tower, leaving gaps of some 25 feet which must presumably have been bridged with wooden planks to afford a continuous passage. It is difficult to see the purpose of this arrangement. In the part north of the main gate these gaps were in later times spanned by arches. This wall dates as a whole to the Hellenistic period, probably to the second century B.C. Along the sea-shore it is almost completely destroyed, and the wall now standing there dates to a re-building in late antiquity.

The Main Gate (B) is also an interesting example of defensive architecture, though its poor state of preservation makes it difficult to appreciate on the ground. The adjoining sketch shows the general layout—a semicircular court (as at Perge and Sillyum) with an outer and an inner gateway, the whole flanked by two large towers in the city-wall. In Roman times, probably about A.D. 200, when the defensive purpose of the gate was no longer of importance, the court was richly ornamented with pillars, niches and statues, in two storeys, of which numerous architectural fragments are lying on the ground. Some of the statues also were found by the excavators and are now in the museum.

In 1965 a second gate (C) in this wall was discovered, not far from the south-east corner. It was completely buried under the sand and was excavated with difficulty; its plan is different

from that of the main gate. It is to be feared that it will before
long be covered over again. The most interesting thing about
this gate is the series of reliefs depicting pieces of armour which
were found on a terrace over the gate, forming a kind of frieze,
and are now arranged along a wall in the museum. The items

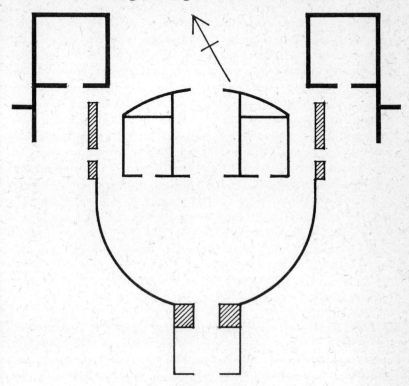

FIG. 16 Side. Plan of the Main Gate

represented are swords, helmets and breastplates. Exhibited
over a gate of the city these must surely be spoils captured
from an enemy, and Professor Mansel has plausibly suggested
that they may commemorate a victory, in the second century
B.C., over Pergamene forces which may have attempted to
occupy Side. No such attack is recorded, but the Nike coins
mentioned above (p. 81) have also been thought to have a
similar significance (Pl. 30).

Opposite the Main Gate, outside the city-wall, is the nymphaeum (X), a building similar in character and purpose to that at Aspendus, but even more splendid. The splendour is now naturally much diminished with the loss of the original marble facing and of the decoration with statues and reliefs, but the monument still stands to more than half its height. The structure consists of a high façade with projecting wings, the whole enclosing a large water-basin. The façade was in three storeys, but little remains of the upper two. The surviving bottom storey contains three large niches, each provided

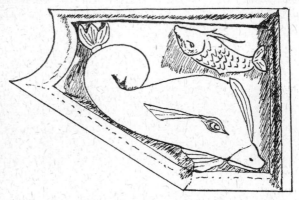

Fig. 17 Side. Relief from the nymphaeum

with three water-spouts; the water was introduced from the rear by a large pipe and conveyed to the spouts by smaller pipes in the wall. How it was brought to this point from the aqueduct is not clear. Many of the architectural fragments found in the excavation are lying around the basin and include a number of handsome reliefs.

The natural sources of water at Side are scanty and of poor quality, and the city was supplied in Roman times by an aqueduct leading from the springs of the river Melas (now the Manavgat Çayı) twenty miles distant. The water was carried partly, and especially in its upper course, by channels and tunnels cut through the rock; in its lower course, and where it crosses dips in the ground, it ran over the high arched structures familiar in Roman times (Pl. 29). It enters the city about

160 yards north of the main gate, where its passage through
the wall may still be seen, and finishes by the inner gateway
close to the theatre. This great work (T on the plan) was
probably constructed at or about the same time as the
nymphaeum, that is, some time in the latter half of the second
century B.C. By the middle of the third century it had fallen
into disrepair and no longer served its purpose; it was restored,
as we learn from inscriptions, by a rich Sidetan citizen,
Bryonianus Lollianus, assisted by contributions from foreigners
of neighbouring cities.

The Main Gate gave its name to one of the four quarters of
the city—at least, the names of four are known from the
inscriptions; there may have been more. They were called after
conspicuous monuments, namely, the Great Gate, the Great
Guild, the Quadriga and the Altar of Zeus. Of these monuments only the first is now to be seen.

From the Great Gate two broad colonnaded streets (E, E)
led into the city. One of these ran southwards, to the left, but
this is now overgrown and difficult to follow; the other leads
straight ahead towards the city centre and the modern village,
and is followed as far as the theatre by the present road. Some
of the columns have been re-erected, but in general the street
is only moderately preserved. At the point, some 400 yards
from the Main Gate, where the street makes a double bend
round the theatre before continuing to the south-west, it was
spanned in Roman times by a high arched gateway (L) which
still stands to a height of over 40 feet and forms one of the
most striking monuments at Side (Pl. 31). It is probable that it
originally carried on its summit a statue of the emperor in a
chariot-and-four, from which the quarter of the Quadriga took
its name; the inscriptions mentioning this quarter were all
found in this neighbourhood. When the size of the city was
reduced about A.D. 400, this became the main entrance; the
arch was blocked up with masonry, through which a smaller
gate was made, with a lintel consisting of a reused marble
block and a relieving arch above. This smaller gate, together
with the masonry above it, has recently been dismantled by
the villagers for fear of collapse, and the appearance of the
whole has greatly suffered.

Just before reaching this inner gate the visitor's eye will be attracted by the newly restored building on the right (H). This is a baths, built probably in the fifth century A.D., when the outer part of the city was reoccupied; it has in the last few years been converted into a museum. The present-day visitor enters at the back through room 5, of which the wall on the street side has disappeared; from here he passes into room 1. These two rooms, like all the others, were originally roofed.

FIG. 18 Side. Inner city gate as it used to be

Room 1 is the Frigidarium; adjoining it is a circular basin, the cold plunge, to which steps lead down. At the north-west end is the main entrance to the baths, originally a double arch, but subsequently modified to its present appearance. The floor is formed of reused marble slabs, some of which carry inscriptions.

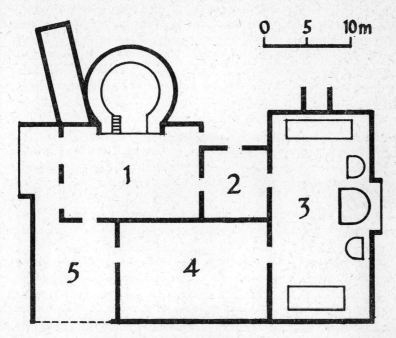

Fig. 19 Side. Baths, now a museum

In the north corner is a narrow room containing a channel which brought the water from the aqueduct. Room 1 was also entered by a small passage in the east corner. It is the only room which was unheated; under each of the others is a hypocaust, that is, the floor was raised on piles of bricks or stones and the space beneath filled with hot air from the furnace. The hottest room of all was room 2, the Sudatorium or sweating-room. The present shape of this room is due to later alteration; it was originally square. The large room 3 was the Caldarium or hot room. The water-basins at either end are original; the other features are later additions. Room 4 was no doubt the Tepidarium or cool room, room 5 the Apodyterium or changing-room. The layout is so arranged that the bather was not obliged to retrace his steps through the rooms he had already used, but emerged from room 4 to room 5 by a door now blocked up.

Directly across the main street from the baths is the agora or market-place F, an open area some 100 yards square, entered from the street by a monumental gateway. Of this, however, and of the agora as a whole, only the foundations now remain. The market-place at Side, as in other ancient cities, served not only as a shopping-centre but also as a meeting-place for the citizens to pass their time. Life in antiquity was spent mostly out of doors, and every day, especially in the mornings, the agora was crowded; 'when the agora is full' was, in fact, the standard expression in Greek for the forenoon. Here, too, in the days of piracy, we may imagine the free men captured by the pirates being sold by auction into slavery.

Round all four sides of the central open square ran a stoa or covered portico, affording shelter in summer from the sun and in winter from the rain. Behind this stood the shops. On the north-west, on either side of the entrance-gate, is a double row of small shops, the outer row opening on to the street, the inner row on to the market-place. On the north-east side is a row of much larger shops. On the south-west, backed against the wall of the stage-building, were nine rooms of which five opened through into the theatre; the other four were perhaps shops. In the west corner, also backed against the theatre, is a large and handsome public latrine of unusual form. It consists of a semicircular arched passage lined with marble, originally containing twenty-four seats with a water-channel beneath. The large niche in the façade facing the agora was merely decorative and probably held statues.

The twenty-odd shops around the agora were, of course, utterly inadequate to the needs of a large city, and remains of many others have been found, not only along the main colon-naded streets but also in the side-streets. It was common in ancient cities to find numerous statues of distinguished persons standing around the market-place; but if this was the case at

Side the statues (and, surprisingly, their bases) have totally disappeared.

Near, but not in, the centre of the agora are the sadly ruined remains of a round building (G) which attracted the attention of the earliest travellers in modern times (Pl. 32). It consisted originally of a circular chamber surrounded by twelve Corinthian columns and surmounted by a roof in the shape of a twelve-sided pyramid. The whole was raised on a podium, or base, of which the core survives, with a flight of steps in front. The ceiling of the central chamber had the form of a dome adorned with the twelve signs of the zodiac. Beaufort in 1812 saw three of the blocks which composed it; they showed, he says, in proper order Pisces, Aries, Taurus, Gemini and Cancer, then surprisingly a swan and a naked young man. Most unfortunately these blocks are now lost. This building is identified with great probability by Professor Mansel as a temple of Tyche, or Fortune. A round temple with pyramidal or conical roof is represented on certain coins of Side of the Roman imperial period, and similar temples on coins of other cities are expressly designated as temples of Tyche. And the signs of the zodiac are obviously appropriate in such a building. Its date is likely to be about the second century A.D.

Just outside the great arched gate, on the left or south side, is an elegant little monument (Z on the plan) whose existence was revealed in the course of removing the masses of blocks which had fallen from the theatre. It has now been partially restored and makes a pleasing addition to the amenities of Side. It consists in its present form of a fountain-house with two water-basins in front, fed by a pipe in the central niche; on either side is a projecting wing supported by columns. But this is not its original form; it was built as a monument to the honour of the emperors Vespasian, whose statue stood in the central niche, and Titus. Enough of the inscription was recovered to date the building to the year A.D. 74.[1] Furthermore, it is virtually certain that the monument, backed against the fourth-century city-wall, is not in its original place. It must

---

[1] It is even possible that the first building was still earlier, and that it was rededicated to Vespasian and Titus; but this depends on an uncertain restoration of the fragmentary inscription.

have stood elsewhere in the city, and was transported to its present position after the wall was constructed, being at the same time converted into a fountain-house. The columns on the wings were originally fluted, like the half-columns in the façade behind them; but they evidently became damaged and were replaced by the present unfluted columns. Fluting was unusual in late antiquity. Two other statues stood one on each side of the niche. One of these was found by the excavators; it shows a male figure, but is too badly damaged to permit any attempt at an identification.

Among all the ruins of Side those of the theatre are outstanding. The building, one of the very largest in Asia Minor, is a conspicuous landmark for miles around (Pl. 34). It dates in its present form to the Roman period, probably the second century A.D. Nothing is known of any earlier theatre, but the shape of the auditorium, considerably exceeding a semicircle, is alone almost conclusive proof that a Hellenistic building previously stood on the site. The ground at Side being almost flat, there was no hillside into which a theatre could be built in the ordinary way; the most that was available was the slight rise to the west of the agora. This barely sufficed to carry the lower half of the auditorium; for the upper part a huge free-standing building was necessary. This still stands about 45 feet high, in two storeys; it was originally some 6 or 8 feet higher. The lower storey consists of a vaulted semicircular corridor supported on massive piers separated by wide openings also vaulted; of these openings some lead through to an inner corridor, others into closed rooms which were perhaps shops or store-rooms. From the inner corridor further openings lead to the diazoma, the horizontal passage which divides the auditorium into equal halves. From here the spectators descended by stairways to reach their seats. Rather surprisingly, there is no communication between the diazoma and the upper seats;[1] these latter were reached by means of narrow interior staircases installed in the thick walls dividing the closed rooms mentioned above, the spectator arriving eventually in the gallery at the extreme top and descending thence to his seat.

[1] The rough steps now in place are merely for the convenience of visitors.

Before the Turkish excavations began the lower part of the auditorium was filled by a forest of trees and bushes, and the stage-building was a heap of collapsed blocks. The latter has now been cleared, but its decoration proves to be sadly battered and broken, and gives only a faint idea of its original appearance. The building is of the Graeco-Roman type familiar in southern Anatolia, and has much in common with the theatre of Aspendus. It is in three storeys rising to a combined height of nearly 70 feet, approximately equal to the total height of the auditorium. The bottom storey is low, only 10 feet high, and projects in front some 20 feet to form the proscenium which was used as a stage. Above this, forming the background, rose the two storeys of the façade, richly decorated with columns, statues, niches and friezes; of this ornamentation many more or less damaged specimens are now lying in the orchestra. At the foot of this façade, at the back of the stage, ran a long frieze with reliefs apparently representing mythological scenes; this frieze is still in place, but the reliefs are so badly damaged as to suggest deliberate destruction in Christian times. (The similar frieze at Perge is much better preserved.) From the nine rooms of the bottom storey five passages, as was mentioned above, led through to the agora; when the inner city-wall was built in the fourth century and the stage-building became a part of the city's fortifications, these passages were naturally blocked up.

The proper purpose of the theatre was, of course, the presentation of plays, but this was not its only use. As populations grew in Hellenistic and especially Roman times, it was found convenient to hold the general assembly of the people, the Ecclesia, in the theatre. Moreover, as the Greeks gradually acquired from the Romans a taste for the more sanguinary gladiatorial shows, fights with wild beasts and the rest, it was felt necessary to stage these also. Their proper setting was the amphitheatre, but very few Greek cities possessed an amphitheatre, and the theatre or the stadium was made to serve. So at Side the orchestra was surrounded, at a comparatively late date, by a 6-foot wall for the protection of the spectators on these occasions.

More remarkably, at a still later date, the theatre seems to have been used as a kind of open sanctuary; at this time two small chapels were installed, one at each corner of the auditorium. Their walls were painted with frescoes, of which some traces may still be seen.

By the fifth century the fabric of the outer corridor had evidently suffered serious damage, apparently from earthquakes, for then or shortly afterwards extensive repairs were undertaken; funds were now available, as the city was enjoying its last period of prosperity. Inscriptions found during the excavation, and now lying between the theatre and the colonnaded street, refer to this work: 'the city', we read, 'at its own expense repaired the piers and arches below the inscription'. The inscription must accordingly have been placed high up above the vaulted openings. The inferior workmanship of the upper parts still shows where these repairs were effected.

Some 150 yards to the south-east of the theatre, just outside the late city-wall, is a building-complex (M on the plan) whose nature and purpose remain something of a mystery. It comprises a large open court, more than 70 yards across, originally surrounded by a colonnade, and on the east side a building containing three large rooms. These rooms, and especially that in the middle, were remarkably richly decorated, as may be judged from the architectural fragments unearthed by the excavators and now lying on the ground (Pl. 36). In the back and side walls were set, in two storeys, alternate niches and projecting bases supporting columns and an entablature; niches and bases both carried statues, of which a considerable number were recovered in a more or less damaged condition and are now in the museum. They are not original works, but copies of classical Greek models, including some of the best-known works of the masters—such, for example, as the Discus-thrower by Myron. An exception, however, is the statue of the Roman emperor, probably Antoninus Pius, which stood in the central niche. A headless statue of Nemesis has been left by the excavators in the niche in the south-east corner. All the walls were veneered with marble; the roof was of wood. The front side of this room was open, apart from a row of six columns.

The adjoining room on the south was a good deal less magnificent; its interior arrangement suggests that it may have been used as a library, but this was not definitely established. The room on the north has not been excavated.

It is very tempting to interpret this building as a gymnasium, especially as no gymnasium has been found elsewhere at Side; it is hardly conceivable that the city did not possess one. The open court, surrounded by a colonnade, has the normal form of a palaestra; if the middle room on the east, with its statue of the emperor, was used for the imperial cult, this, too, would be perfectly normal—as, for example, in the gymnasium at Pergamum. But there are difficulties, in particular the absence of the usual smaller rooms both for athletic purposes (coating with sand, anointing with oil, etc.) and for educational purposes; for the ancient gymnasium served also as a school or university. Above all, the total absence of any bathing facilities is an almost fatal drawback. Most gymnasia in Roman times had full-scale hot baths (Thermae) adjoining; but here even the simpler Greek wash-room is lacking. The alternative suggested by the excavators is that we have a second agora, not in this case a market but merely a place of public resort. A library, and a hall assigned to the cult of the emperor, would be appropriate enough as adjuncts to such a public square.

Beyond the theatre the main colonnaded street diverges from the present road and runs southward for 500 yards almost to the shore; but since it passes through the outlying parts of the modern village this stretch has not been excavated. At its southern end, on the east side, are the remains of a building of elegant construction, though now badly ruined (S on the plan). It consists of a semicircular chamber facing west, with a platform in front which originally carried six columns with entablature; the whole is raised on a base about 7 feet high, which is still preserved, and approached by a flight of steps. It is thought to be a temple, and some rather uncertain indications suggest that it may have been dedicated to the Anatolian moon-god Men. At all events, the western aspect tends to show that it did not belong to any of the Olympian deities, whose temples were normally entered from the east. Its date is probably not far from A.D. 200.

At the southern extremity of the peninsula, side by side on a levelled platform, stood the two principal temples of the city (P and Q on the plan). Little more than the foundations now survives, though enough architectural fragments of Q were found to permit a restoration on paper. Apart from a difference in size, the two buildings are virtually twins. Each was in the Corinthian order, with a single row of columns numbering eleven on the sides and six at front and back. Each had a front chamber, or pronaos, entered between two columns, and a main chamber, or cella, but in each the rear chamber, or opisthodomus, is lacking. In the case of Q the plan is quite clearly distinguishable on the ground; P is more thoroughly destroyed. These two are by far the largest and (originally) most impressive temples yet discovered at Side; the excavation produced no actual evidence to show to what gods they belonged, but it is reasonable to attribute them to the principal deities of the city, Athena and Apollo (Pl. 40).

By their artistic style these temples may be dated to the latter part of the second century A.D. A recently discovered inscription of similar date records the name of a victor at a festival having the curious title 'Landing-Festival of Athena'; and a series of third-century inscriptions relates to the 'Landing-Festival of Athena and Apollo'. This has been explained as referring to these deities, in their temples by the harbour, as watchers over the safe arrival of shipping in the port of Side. This hardly seems, however, to afford an occasion for an athletic festival, and in the present writer's opinion a more attractive explanation is possible. When the new temples were completed they would, of course, need cult-statues, and these would very probably be commissioned from abroad. When the ship carrying them arrived in the harbour of Side we may well imagine that a public holiday would be proclaimed; it is easy to picture the ship, gaily decorated, sailing in, the cheering crowds of citizens, the landing of the statues and their ceremonial installation in the neighbouring temples. What better occasion for the establishment of a festival with games? Since Apollo's name was added later, it seems that his temple was finished, or at least his statue arrived, after that of Athena.

In Byzantine times a large basilica was built immediately

29   Side. The Aqueduct by the Homa Road

30   Side. Reliefs showing enemy spoils, from the south-east
          gate.

31   Side. Inner City-Gate and Monument of Vespasian.

32   Side. The Agora, with Round Temple, Street and Baths
           (Museum), from the Theatre.

33   Side. Side-street by the Baths.

34   Side. The Theatre.

35   Side. The Gymnasium (?).

36   Side. Ceiling-block from the Gymnasium (?).

37   Side. Relief found during the excavation.

38   Side. Tragic Mask from the Theatre.

39   Side. Monument of Modesta, with reliefs of
      gladiatorial shows given by her.

40   Side. The Temples by the Harbour.

42   Alânya. The Dockyard.

41   Side. The Mausoleum by the shore.

43   Alânya. The Red Tower from the Dockyard.

44   Alânya. View from the Castle.

[*opposite*]

45   Alânya. Seljuk Fortification and Hellenistic Wall.

46   Alânya. The Castle Ramparts.

47   Alânya. The Caravanserai.

52   Evdir Hanı. The Seljuk Doorway.

[*opposite*]

50   Magydus. Falls of the Düden Su.

51   Olbia (?). Medieval Bridge over the Arapsu.

53   Evdir Hanı. Carving at the Temple.

54   Seleuceia. The Market-Building.

to the east of the two temples; much of it is still standing. In front of it a great forecourt was planned to occupy the temple-platform. For this purpose temple P, which must presumably have fallen by then into a ruinous state, was completely removed, except that its northern row of columns was permitted to survive as an ornament to the forecourt; some drums of these are still lying on the ground. The northern side of the court was formed by the solid wall, with niches, which still stands; the corresponding southern side would have passed through the middle of Q, but for some reason this was not carried out, and it appears that this temple survived longer than the other; for this reason its destruction is less complete.

Apart from the three just mentioned, only two other temple-buildings have been identified at Side. One of these is the round temple of Tyche in the agora; the other is a small building (J on the plan) between the theatre and the main street, close to the inner city-gate. Only a part of the base (podium) survives, but the plan of the temple is recoverable; its most remarkable feature is that it was not surrounded as usual by a row of free-standing columns, but had instead half-columns set against the cella walls. This style, known technically as pseudoperipteral, is familiar in the west—the Maison Carrée at Nîmes is a well-known example—but seems not to occur elsewhere in Asia Minor. From its proximity to the theatre we may with some probability assign this temple to Dionysus.

But there were certainly other temples at Side besides these. In particular the city must have possessed buildings devoted to the cult of the emperors, whose priests are frequently mentioned in the inscriptions. Indeed, as was said above, Side boasted the title of 'Six times Temple-Warden', and of these six some at least must have been temples of the emperors. The title Neocorus was originally, in the early days of the empire, granted only in respect of the imperial cult; but by the second and third centuries we find it given also in connexion with the principal deities of the individual cities. So at Side it is likely that the temples of Athena and Apollo conferred this distinction. In addition, the inscriptions record priests of numerous other deities, among them Zeus, Poseidon, Aphrodite and the Egyptian Sarapis.

FIG. 21 Sarcophagus at Side

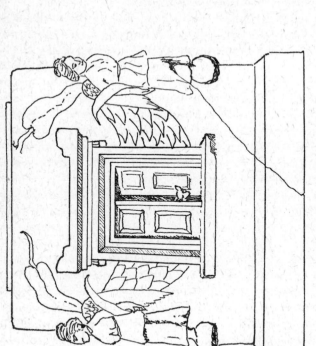

FIG. 20 Sarcophagus at Side

The necropolis lay, as usual, outside the city-walls and covered a wide area now occupied by cultivated fields. The types of tomb vary greatly. The grandest of all is a mausoleum by the shore about a quarter of a mile to the west of the city, in the direction of the new motel. The tomb was in the form of a temple raised on a base, or podium, and surrounded by a courtyard; though badly ruined, and to a large extent built of reused materials, it still impresses both by its size and by the richness of its ornamentation. In front, a much larger court-yard extended all the way to the shore. This grandiose complex appears to have been constructed towards A.D. 300, but the name of the occupant is not known (Pl. 41).

Nearer to the city a number of handsome sarcophagi were unearthed and are now in the museum. Two of them are illustrated in Figs. 20 and 21. In the former the chief feature is a double door of the usual ancient type, flanked on either side at the corners of the sarcophagus by two winged figures of Victory, each holding a palm-branch. The door is ajar and a dog looks out, the faithful guardian of the tomb as he formerly was of the house. This charming motif is rare, if not unknown, elsewhere. The other tomb is that of a woman, and again the centre is occupied by a double door. At its foot rests the owner's fan, and to right and left are her wool-basket and spindle. Above these the swallow and butterfly symbolise the mourning for the soul on its passage to the other world.[1] The wreaths of olive-branches have much the same significance as the wreaths of flowers familiar today. This sarcophagus has been reused, and, inappropriately enough, by a man. The original inscription has been erased and the man's name, Ctetus Dionysius, substituted, while the feminine attributes have been left untouched.

The harbour of Side lies beyond the village at the end of the promontory. The Pamphylian coast is virtually devoid of natural harbours, and that of Side is almost wholly artificial. Not only was a powerful mole required to make it usable at all, but the basin itself needed to be largely dug out. The passage through the middle of the mole is about 30 feet wide, but may originally have been wider; it was notorious as a

---

[1] *Psyche*, 'the soul', is also the Greek for a butterfly.

difficult entrance. The water is very shallow, and the inner half of the harbour, like the eastern part of the city, has become completely sanded up. Even in antiquity this process gave continual trouble, and it was repeatedly necessary to dredge the basin; so much so that the expression 'It's a regular harbour of Side' became proverbial for a task that perpetually needed to be done over again. An inscription of about A.D. 300 honours a certain provincial governor who performed this service. The task could never be neglected, for in spite of all difficulties the harbour was essential to the city's prosperity; throughout its history Side lived by its maritime commerce, and even after the foundation of Attaleia competed vigorously to be the leading port of Pamphylia.

*

CHAPTER SEVEN

Alânya (Coracesium)

OF ALL the ancient sites along the Pamphylian and Cilician coasts by far the most impressive is the great rock of Alânya. Over 800 feet high, it projects boldly into the sea and makes a mighty landmark from afar. Yet the city, Coracesium, which occupied it in antiquity was never of much account; apart from its ability to resist capture, it is chiefly noted as a headquarters of the Cilician pirates. The geographical treatise which passes under the name of Scylax records its existence in the mid-fourth century, while the country was still in Persian control, but nothing is known of its early history.

When Antiochus III of Syria, about 197 B.C., was successfully campaigning to recover the Cilician coast, Coracesium was the only place to hold out against him. It was presumably occupied by a Ptolemaic garrison, and we may fairly infer that the Hellenistic fortifications, of which some remnants survive, were then in existence.

Some fifty years later a certain Diodotus, surnamed Tryphon, the Voluptuary, in the course of his revolt against Antiochus VII, used Coracesium as his headquarters. He it was who, according to Strabo, initiated the practice of piracy which soon became such a serious menace. When the Romans finally sent Pompey to deal with it, the climax of his campaign was a sea-battle off Coracesium, in which the pirates were crushed once for all. Later, when Antony, after the murder of Caesar, was in control of the east, he presented the city and the surrounding territory to Cleopatra; timber was always scarce in Egypt, and the cedar-wood which was floated down the Dim Çayı and the Kargı Çayı was valuable to the queen for the construction of her navies.

Reckoned sometimes as the last city of Pamphylia,

101

sometimes as the first of Cilicia, Coracesium flourished in a modest way through the period of the empire. About A.D. 100, under Trajan, it struck its own coins for the first time; this may indicate an upgrading of the city's status. Later it was the seat of a bishopric, under the metropolitan of Side. Of this early town nothing now remains but some pieces of the wall and three or four inscriptions found in the neighbouring villages.

The name Coracesium did not survive. In Byzantine times it was changed to Kalonoros, 'the Fine Mountain', and this name continued as Candiloro, or in other corrupted forms, in the Italian and Greek portolans at least down to the sixteenth century, long after the Moslem occupation.

As the Byzantine emperors' hold on the south coast weakened, and especially after the advent of the Seljuk Turks in the eleventh century, a number of Armenian chieftains established independent dynasties at various places, one of which was Kalonoros. Not until the early thirteenth century did the Seljuks reach the Cilician coast. In 1221 Keykûbad I (1219–34) attacked Kalonoros, but found it a far from easy prey; indeed, he only succeeded in occupying it when its Armenian governor was persuaded to surrender it peaceably in exchange for a principality elsewhere.

Keykûbad then renamed the town Alâiye, 'city of Alâ', with reference to the title of Alâ-üd-din which he had assumed on his accession.[1] He then proceeded to construct the magnificent fortifications which stand essentially unchanged today. Keykûbad set considerable store by his splendid new city and made it not only an almost impregnable fortress but also something of a cultural centre; and in the commercial sphere he established a sugar factory there, while the export of timber to Egypt continued as in the time of Cleopatra.

Following the breakdown of the Seljuk domination at the end of the thirteenth century something of the splendour was lost, and unsettled times began. Alâiye came at different periods under the Gazi dynasties of Karamanoğlu and Tekkeoğlu, and entered into varying relations with the kings of Cyprus. When the Turkish traveller Evliya Çelebi came to the town in 1671 he found it a good deal reduced, but still equipped with

[1] The 'n' in the modern name is intrusive.

schools, shops, caravanserais and baths; he was particularly impressed by the fortifications. He notes incidentally that by order of the Sultan the inhabitants were authorised to kill on sight any Frank, Armenian or Jew; but the Greeks were tolerated and established in a quarter of their own. At this time Alâiye was attached to the Beylerbey of Adana.

The deterioration continued, and Beaufort in 1811 found only an unimportant town with miserable streets and houses. The revival of Alânya to its present condition of modest prosperity is the work of the Turkish government in quite recent times.

The castle hill, precipitous on the south and west, descends on the north-east by a steep but practicable slope to the harbour. This slope is occupied by houses picturesquely set among the walls and trees. On the shore the visitor's eye is at once attracted by two conspicuous buildings, the old dockyard and the Red Tower.

The latter of these, called in Turkish *Kızıl Kule* (A on the plan), is shown by its inscription to be among the earliest buildings erected by Keykûbad. From outside one sees a plain octagonal tower with a crenellated parapet and projecting machicolations for dropping missiles upon an enemy (Pl. 43, 44). The interior is more complicated, with five storeys each having a different arrangement. The central pier contains a water-cistern with its mouth on the fourth floor. The remarkably complete appearance of this tower is due to skilful Turkish restoration in 1951–3. Near the Red Tower is a fountain which supplies the only running water on the hill; for the rest the population was dependent on rainwater cisterns, of which there are said to be 400, 100 of them still in use.

Some 200 yards along the shore to the south, and well worth a visit, is the dockyard, or *Tersane* (B), designed for the construction of ships and still used for the building and storing of small boats. It consists of five vaulted galleries side by side, with arched openings in the walls between them (Pl. 42). The entrance is on the north, with a room on either side, probably a store-house and an office respectively. The dockyard is guarded on the south side by a tower (P) known as *Tophane*, 'the arsenal'.

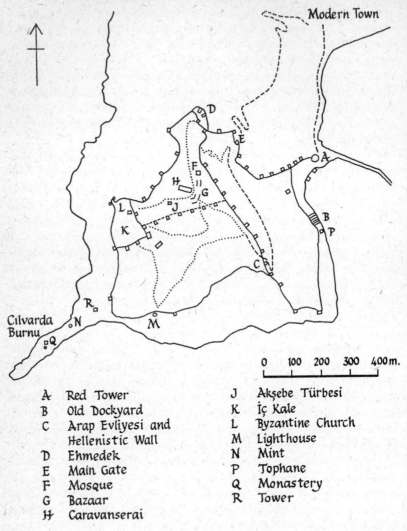

Cılvarda
Burnu

A	Red Tower	
B	Old Dockyard	
C	Arap Evliyesi and	
	Hellenistic Wall	
D	Ehmedek	
E	Main Gate	
F	Mosque	
G	Bazaar	
H	Caravanserai	
J	Akşebe Türbesi	
K	İç Kale	
L	Byzantine Church	
M	Lighthouse	
N	Mint	
P	Tophane	
Q	Monastery	
R	Tower	

FIG. 22 Plan of Alânya

104

From the Red Tower the fortification-wall runs up to the northern fortress D, called Ehmedek. This stretch protects the most vulnerable part, and is especially strongly defended not only by towers but with a second, outer wall and a dry ditch. It contains the principal gate (E), to which the motor-road leads up. This is really two gates, one in the outer wall and the main gatehouse in the inner wall, so arranged that in entering two right-angled turns are necessary. Beside the outer gate the wall is decorated with a painted check pattern of red and white squares. The arch under which the road now passes has been made recently for the convenience of visitors with cars.

Inside the castle the motor-road runs southward for some 500 yards, then turns back and winds circuitously up to the top of the hill; it is at present rough and stony. But the visitor who desires to see more than the view from the summit is strongly recommended to leave his car at or near this turn and make his way on foot by the narrow lanes and paths among the trees and houses to the various points of interest. Merely to drive to the top and down again is to miss nearly all the charm of the old town.

Near where the road makes this first turn the Seljuk wall may be seen resting on eight or nine courses of the old Hellenistic wall of Coracesium, which ran up from here to the Ehmedek; it is constructed of good solid ashlar masonry (Pl. 45). Over the ruins of a tower in this wall a Byzantine chapel was built; it is now known as Arap Evliyesi and survives in very fair condition (C on the plan). Alâ-üd-din was indeed careful not to injure it when he rebuilt the wall. In general the Turks have never been wantonly destructive of older buildings; for the most part they preferred to convert them to their own use.

At the north end of this wall is the Ehmedek (D), a fortress also used for residential purposes. The main approach from the south-east leads over the ditch and through a door in the outer wall to a gatehouse of the usual type, with a right-angled turn on entering. Just inside is a courtyard with cisterns, and to the left a stepped path leads up to the ruins of three towers which formed the termination of the Hellenistic wall. Ahead and to the right are three more towers of Seljuk construction; the middle one contains in one corner a small chamber which has been identified as a bathroom. The southern tower is now ruined.

A path leads south from the Ehmedek to a group of buildings which seems to have formed the centre of the Seljuk city.[1] The Süleymaniye Mosque (F) is a simple square building with a porch on the north side and a cistern attached to one corner. The conical shelter at the top of the minaret is a modern addition replacing the damaged original.

Immediately to the south of this is a bazaar, or *Bedesten* (G), in a fair state of preservation, and adjoining this on the west is a well-preserved *Han*, or caravanserai (H). The rectangular courtyard is surrounded by chambers affording accommodation for the visiting merchants, and a large vaulted extension at the back was for stabling their animals (Pl. 47).

By a path which leads up from here to the west is an interesting little building (J) known as the Akşebe Türbesi. It seems to have combined the functions of a *türbe*, or tomb, and a *mescit*, or small mosque, and has some unusual features. The *mescit* is a square domed chamber with three openings in its north wall, of which the middle one is surprisingly high and narrow. Adjoining on the east is a sort of annexe, comprising a second domed chamber and a small room which seems to have served as the *türbe*. At present both rooms are occupied by tombs. This second chamber has a separate entrance by a large open arch, and does not communicate with the *mescit*. A minaret stands isolated on the north-west (Pl. 49).

Continuing up the path to the west the visitor reaches the highest point of the hill. Here is the citadel of Alâiye, known as the İç Kale or Inner Castle (K). It consists of an open space some 200 yards long, strongly defended on three sides, less strongly on the west, where the cliffs are precipitous. This citadel is curiously lacking in buildings of importance; indeed, the most conspicuous is, surprisingly enough, a handsome little Byzantine church (L). The other buildings seem to be mere barracks ranged along the walls. The entrance was in the

---

[1] Walking up from C to the Ehmedek the visitor will pass these on the way.

middle of the east side (not where it is now), with the usual right-angled turn. At the north-west corner is the spot which has been identified, somewhat uncertainly, with the so-called *Adam atacağı*, or 'place from which men may be thrown'. Otherwise the chief feature of the İç Kale is the numerous large water-tanks, at least seven in number.

Finally, mention may be made of the curious rocky tongue which extends from the south-west corner of the hill some 300 or 400 yards into the sea. It is called the Cılvarda Burnu, and carries the ruins of three buildings. The first and most conspicuous is the tower R; the second (N) is identified as the Darphane, or mint, but it is hard to believe that a mint would be established in so inaccessible a spot. It is now quite destroyed. The third (Q) is a monastery with associated buildings, and may be reached with difficulty by landing in a boat on the west side of the promontory. Between N and Q is an impassable rift in the rock; and the descent from the castle above is highly dangerous except to an experienced alpinist.

Among the amenities of Alânya is the stalactite cave, known as Damlataş, adjoining the bathing beach at the foot of the castle hill on the west side. Discovered by chance in 1948, it is reckoned beneficial to sufferers from rheumatism, numbers of whom may generally be found sitting for long hours in the cave. When the writer recently visited it the temperature inside was 73°F. and the humidity 96 per cent.

There are also several other ancient sites in the neighbourhood of Alânya which the enterprising traveller might consider visiting, though they cannot be fully described here. Five miles to the north-west of Alânya, on a hill above the village of Elikesik, are the ruins which are probably those of Hamaxia. The ring-wall is fairly well preserved; in the interior are some remains of buildings among dense trees and undergrowth. Ten miles to the east, high up on the slopes of Cebelireş, the highest mountain of the region, is another city which is perhaps Laertes, home of the writer Diogenes Laertius. Further to the east, on the summit of the first promontory along the coast from Alânya, are the ruins of Syedra. None of these sites has anything very remarkable to offer the visitor, beyond the charm which is inseparable from any remote and deserted ancient city.

★

CHAPTER EIGHT

Minor Sites and Excursions

MAGYDUS AND OLBIA

BEFORE Attaleia existed the western end of the Pamphylian plain was occupied by the two towns of Olbia and Magydus. Both are mentioned from the fourth century B.C. onwards, but the foundation of Attaleia greatly reduced their importance; neither town has any history to speak of, and today even their sites are not determined with certainty. From the ancient notices it appears that Olbia lay to the west of Attaleia, Magydus to the east.

For Magydus the site generally accepted is at Lara, about five miles from the centre of Antalya, between the bathing-beach and the military base to the west; it is at present partly occupied by a small NATO establishment. The chief feature of the site is the artificial harbour, some 250 yards in length and breadth (Pl. 48). On the west side the ancient mole is preserved for some distance above the surface, then continues round under water, reappearing at one point only; the entrance is just to the west of this point. On the shore are numerous remains of ancient buildings, all of late date and poor masonry with lavish use of mortar; the most striking is a baths, still standing some 20 feet high and occupied at the time of writing by a Turkish family. Just below this is a spring of good water, said to be very health-giving. Along the beach is a row of buildings side by side; these are likely to have been shops or warehouses. Down the gentle slope behind runs an aqueduct with an open channel; its water was perhaps drawn from the neighbouring Düden Su, which falls over a cliff into the sea in a fine cascade about a mile to the west (Pl. 50). Various cut blocks and column-stumps are lying scattered on the slope.

That this site does indeed represent Magydus seems to the present writer to be very probable. The good-sized artificial harbour seems a sure indication of a settlement earlier than Attaleia; after the foundation of that port it is unlikely that another would be constructed so close to it. Nor is the late date of the extant remains a fatal objection, for Magydus seems to have attained city-status at a comparatively late period; its coins begin only in the time of Domitian (A.D. 81–96) and continue till the middle of the third century. Moreover, Magydus is associated by the ancient geographers with the river Catarrhactes, which is unquestionably the Düden Su. No inscriptions or finds of coins have yet come to confirm the identification, but no site along this coast has been found which offers a reasonable alternative.

Olbia, on the other hand, remains something of a mystery. It is mentioned in the fourth century by the pseudo-Scylax and by Aristotle, and there is no reason to doubt that it was founded with the others at the time of the early migration. It seems to have been sufficiently prosperous to send out a colony; at least, we are told that Cadrema in Lycia was a foundation of the Olbians. There were other cities called Olbia, but as a founder of a colony in Lycia ours is much the most likely. Concerning Cadrema we have no other information whatever. By Strabo's time Olbia was much reduced; he calls it merely 'a mighty bastion', and it seems improbable that it then had city-status; at all events it struck no coins under the empire as the other cities did. A chief reason for this decline was almost certainly the foundation of Attaleia; it is not unlikely that Attalus manned his new city in part with the men of Olbia. A place of some sort was surviving in the fifth century, but no bishop of Olbia is recorded. Olbia was a city that lived its good days early.

For the site Strabo gives us precise information. He calls Olbia 'the beginning of Pamphylia', and locates it 367 stades from Cape Hiera, that is the cape at the south-east corner of Lycia, now called Gelidonya Burnu.[1] Three hundred and sixty-seven stades is sixty-six kilometres or forty-one miles, and this leads, in fact, to the western extremity of the Pamphylian

[1] From the Chelidonian Islands, now Beşadalar, just off the point.

plain.[1] Unfortunately there seems to be no site thereabouts which can be confidently identified with Olbia.

Various suggestions have been put forward. Lieutenant Spratt's companion Daniell believed he had found the site at a point above the left bank of the Çandır river about nine miles from the sea, where he saw extensive remains on the steep mountainside. Spratt himself, however, preferred an utterly different site only three or four miles west of Antalya, close to the mouth of the Arapsu river.[2]

From Antalya to the west the country extends in the form of a rocky plateau, which after a mile or two breaks down into a series of low hills like inland promontories, flat-topped, steep-sided and largely covered with scrub. Spratt's site, which he himself discovered, is on one of these. It is most easily reached by following the left (east) bank of the river as well as possible through the fields and orchards for about 500 yards from the road, to a narrow gorge through which the stream passes. The hill on the east side of this gorge is the one in question; there is an easy way up from the stream. The surface of this hill is flat and rocky, but less encumbered by scrub than most of the others; despite the unattractive nature of the ground, foundations of walls and houses may be seen here and there, and at the north-east end the hill is barred from side to side by the massive wall which first attracted Spratt's attention. Only one or two courses now remain, and even these are in danger, as a lime-kiln is established on the line of the wall.[3] The masonry is an irregular ashlar and the blocks are of good size; two which the writer noticed measure 4 feet 3 inches by 2 feet and 2 feet 10 inches by 2 feet 8 inches respectively. Even more remarkable is the thickness of the wall, which is no less than 14 feet. The blocks are fitted without mortar, and there can be no doubt that the wall is of a very respectable antiquity; it is built in the familiar ancient fashion with an inner and an outer face and rubble filling. At

[1] Strabo's account obviously excludes Antalya as the site of Olbia; see above, p. 41.
[2] The Arapsu is the first stream along the coast road passing the Konyaaltı bathing-beach.
[3] This kiln is conspicuous and makes a convenient landmark for finding the wall.

its east end the wall makes a short return to the south, and just outside is a narrow ancient road cut in the rock, with wheel-ruts visible here and there. Numerous other walls are standing on the site, but they are all of very late date, thin and of wretched masonry with abundant mortar. In the gorge on the west, walls and buildings of this kind may be seen on either side of the stream, and the stream itself is crossed by an old bridge which is still sound and in regular use as a footbridge. Spratt calls it 'ancient', but the shallow pointed arch betrays its post-Roman date (Pl. 51). Below the bridge the river-banks are lined with walls of squared blocks not unlike those of the massive wall on the hill above, but rather smaller. Some 200 yards above the bridge, in the cliff on the west bank, is a group of about twenty tombs of semicircular 'arcosolium' type, which might well be of Roman date, and other plain rock-tombs may be seen on either side of the gorge. The whole site is very attractive and makes a pleasant little excursion from Antalya, especially in the spring, when the country is still fresh and green. Whether it can really be the site of Olbia is much more doubtful. That there was occupation of some sort in early times the great wall is enough to prove; but the site bears little resemblance to those normally chosen by the early settlers, and it is more like fifty than forty miles from Gelidonya Burnu. Spratt was content to accept it as answering to Strabo's 'mighty bastion', but he certainly over-estimated its strength; he reckoned the height of the cliffs in the gorge as 70 or 80 feet, but the true figure is nearer 40 or 50, and on the other sides it is even less than this. Most people will feel that something more impressive would be expected.

A third proposal has recently found some favour. Close above the village of Kurma, or Gurma, at the very extremity of the plain, is a bold and steep rocky hill a little way back from the shore. This is said to carry the ruins of one or two buildings, called by the locals 'churches', which the present writer has not seen; they do not appear to amount to much of a site. Spratt suggested that this might represent the Olbian colony Cad-rema. A few miles to the west, close below the present road that leads over the mountains to Finike, are several sarcophagi of Lycian type and some traces of buildings, but these cannot indicate more than a village site at the most. The place is called Kocaköy.

The problem therefore remains. Not a single inscription of any help has been found on any of the sites proposed. The Kurma rock exactly suits Strabo's estimate of distance, and moreover admirably answers to his description as a mighty bastion; if it offered something more like an ancient city there would be no hesitation in accepting it.

EVDİR HANI

On the road from Antalya to Termessus and Korkuteli, four and a half miles from the point where this diverges from the Burdur road, is the coffee-house of Uzunkuyu; 100 yards before the bridge over the stream a narrow road, just passable for motor traffic, leads north to the Evdir Hanı. This is a fine specimen of a Seljuk caravanserai, above average size, with a particularly handsome entrance on the south side (Pl. 52). It was built by Sultan Keykâvus about the end of the thirteenth century.

Between the *han* and the main road are the scattered ruins of an ancient town or large village; to visit these it is best to take a guide from the coffee-house, as it is not easy to find one's way among the modern houses and fields. The most striking peculiarity of the site is the large number of water-channels which intersect it at right-angles; as at Perge, their containing-walls have become overlaid with a deposit of lime. The main channel, which passes close to the *han* on the west, is still in use today, and has been for the last thirty years, needing no repair or maintenance beyond keeping the passage clear. The writer was informed that once a week or thereabouts water is carried down by this channel from the neighbourhood of the Kırkgöz Hanı, some eight miles to the north, for purposes of irrigation.

In general there is less to see on the site now than there was in Spratt's time, for much has disappeared with the recent growth of the village. Of the hundreds of sarcophagi that he saw in 1842 quite a number survive, but they are largely buried or broken. In the southern part of the site, not far from the coffee-house, are the heaped ruins of a small temple which was once exceedingly handsome. Huge epistyle blocks richly decorated, spiral-fluted column-drums and coffered ceiling-blocks are lying around; and beside the building lies the curious figure shown on Pl. 53, with another similar to it close by.

The ancient name of this site is not known with certainty. Spratt's idea that it was the city of Lagon was due merely to misunderstanding of an inscription that he found there; it has unfortunately been adopted, through an oversight, by Freya Stark. It is certain that the place was never an independent city; its position, and the fact that in some of the inscriptions on the sarcophagi the fine for violation is made payable to Solymian Zeus,[1] leave no doubt that it was a dependency of Termessus. It is likely, though not proved, that in the fifth century it received the name of Eudocias, in honour of Eudoxia, wife of the Emperor Theodosius II; Eudocias is commonly associated with Termessus in the Byzantine lists of bishoprics. As for its earlier name, it is possible, though again unproved, that it was called Anydrus, 'Waterless'; a village of this name is mentioned in the inscriptions of Termessus, and lack of water would afford a natural reason for constructing the numerous channels to bring it from outside.

VARSAK

The step which divides the Pamphylian plain into two levels was mentioned above. At the foot of the cliffs forming this step, about seven miles due north of Antalya, is the village of Varsak, accessible by a moderate road. On the level plateau above the cliffs is an extensive ancient village site now known as Ören Mevkii or Ören Gediği. Spread over a considerable area are numerous remains of houses and other buildings; from the quality of the masonry they may be dated to the Roman imperial period. Close by is an equally extensive necropolis containing sarcophagi and handsome built tombs, but for the most part these are badly damaged. From an inscription built into a wall at the west end of the site we learn

[1] Below, pp. 120, 131, 135.

that it was known in antiquity as the 'Village of the Lyrbotae', and that Apollo was worshipped here under the title of 'Apollo of the Lyrbotae'.

Further to the west there is another, smaller site called Çaylak. It is reached by a delightful walk through pine-woods, but the actual ruins are of no significance.

SELEUCEIA IN PAMPHYLIA

Seven miles due north of Manavgat, and one hour's walk from the village of Şıhlar, are the ruins of a small city which has been surprisingly neglected. Surprisingly, because it is quite easily reached and the standing remains are distinctly impressive. It has been identified, correctly in the writer's opinion, with the Pamphylian Seleuceia, a minor city of which very little is heard in the ancient authors. The map of Asia Minor is quite thickly strewn with cities by the name of Seleuceia, called after the various kings Seleucus of Syria. The best known is the Cilician, further along the coast, which has preserved its ancient name in the form Silifke.

The site is of a type much favoured in antiquity, a hill precipitous on three sides and accessible only on the south. The visitor approaching from Şıhlar comes first to a narrow col formerly barred by a wall and gate. Just inside this, in a hollow on the left, is a fine spring of water, shaded by fig-trees, issuing from a cave, with remains of ancient masonry indicating an artificial pool. A little above this spring is a large building still 30 feet high, which makes a landmark visible for several miles to the south. It consists of five vaulted rooms side by side, and was evidently a baths; the round holes for water-pipes may still be seen in the walls.

The city-centre (Fig. 23) is towards the east near the foot of the hill. Here is the agora, surrounded by buildings in a remarkable state of preservation. The most striking is the market-hall on the east side (Pl. 54), in two storeys of which the lower is virtually complete; of the upper storey much of the front wall survives, with large rectangular windows. The lower floor contains a row of eight compartments; six of these are shops, and have doors with horizontal lintel. The end compartment on the north, which has an arched doorway, has its floor at a much lower level than the rest; the reason for this is not clear. The fourth door from the north is also arched and led to a stairway, now destroyed, giving access by a door at the back to the upper storey.

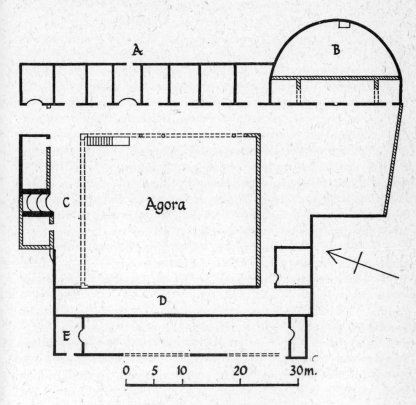

FIG. 23 Seleuceia. The city centre

Adjoining this building on the south is a semicircular structure (B) which appears to have been a later addition. Its purpose is uncertain; a council house and an odeum have been suggested. It is likely to have had seating, though none now remains; perhaps it was of wood. The rough wall across the interior, and the beam-holes in the front wall, suggest a subsequent conversion into additional shops. The building is entered by four doors; over the second from the south is cut an inscription recording that it was built by a certain Nectarius, of whom nothing is known.

The agora was, as usual, surrounded by a colonnade; some of the columns on the east side are still standing in part. The rough staircase at the north-east corner seems at present rather meaningless. On the north side, in the middle, is a vaulted entrance passage (C), now blocked at its north end; this is flanked on the east by a building of handsome masonry, and on the west by another building now destroyed.

On the west side the ground is lower and a basement storey (D) was necessary; this is quite well preserved and has shallow arched recesses on either side. The small building E at the north-west corner is also well preserved, with handsome cushioned masonry. At the south-west corner the ground falls steeply away, and here the wall is standing to nearly 50 feet; its lower part is built of fine bossed masonry.

A little to the north of the market-hall, beyond the area shown on the plan, is a small temple, also in good preservation; the cella is standing complete, apart, of course, from its roof. In its interior walls are arched niches which appear, from the holes and grooves cut in them, to have been closed with grilles; they may perhaps have held the temple treasures. There was apparently a row of four columns in front, but these have now gone.

The necropolis is near the western edge of the hill. The tombs are mostly built of masonry, and one remarkable group contained two horizontal rows of six, one above the other, but not all of these are preserved.

PART THREE

Pisidia

*

CHAPTER NINE

Termessus

RATHER LESS than twenty miles to the north-west of Antalya the Korkuteli road enters a defile leading to a high pass some ten miles further on. In the defile, by the roadside, is a coffee-house known as Yenice Kahve; high above this, on the mountain to the south (the Güllük Dağ), are the ruins of Termessus. From the coffee-house a path leads up by a long and gradual slope; on foot it is two hours from the road to the city-centre; but a good motor-road has recently been construc-ted which goes as far as a small clearing, from which it is a bare half-hour's climb to the principal ruins.

Termessus, perched on and around the summit of its mountain, a subsidiary peak of the Güllük Dağ, 3,500 feet above sea-level and buried in forest and undergrowth, has an utterly different atmosphere from the cities of the plain. Not that the ruins themselves are so very different: they belong in the main, as elsewhere, to the Roman period and include the normal types of building: but the mountain air and the remoteness of the site, combined with the excellent preserva-tion of many of the monuments, make a visit to Termessus altogether delightful. It is true that at present it is difficult to get about, and the visitor can easily find himself temporarily lost; but few will probably be deterred by this.[1]

In its origin Termessus was not a Greek city; the 'mixed multitude' who settled in the plain below never found their way up here. The place was first occupied by Pisidian barbar-ians, and the city was always reckoned Pisidian; when it is called a city of Pamphylia this has no reference to any racial connexion with the men of Perge or Aspendus, but merely to

---

[1] There is said to be an intention to clear the site in the near future, at least enough to make the main buildings comfortably accessible.

the fact that it was included in the Roman province of Pamphylia. The ancient name of Güllük Dağ was Solymus, and the Termessians in their inscriptions allude to themselves as Solymians; they seem to have spoken a dialect of Pisidian which Strabo calls Solymian and distinguishes from the language spoken in Pisidia. But the city was Hellenised at a date earlier than any of its surviving inscriptions, and no trace now remains of the Solymian dialect apart from the names of its citizens. Many of these are indeed strange names not found elsewhere: Kismis, Piaterabis, Sampsys, Kodnoundis and many others. Greeks and Anatolians, unlike the Romans, had normally only one name; many of the Anatolian names, such as Obrangoueis, Kbarolasis, Saralougeris, seem to us clumsy, and can hardly have been convenient for familiar use.

At what date Termessus was founded is not known, but the Solymians appear as early as Homer, in connexion with the romantic story of Bellerophon. This young man had the misfortune to play the part of Joseph in the tale of Potiphar's wife; loved and falsely accused by the wife of Proetus king of Argos, he was sent by the latter to the court of Iobates in Lycia, carrying with him a sealed letter requesting that he be put to death. By way of executing this commission Iobates set him to destroy the monstrous Chimaera; on his return unexpectedly successful he was next sent to fight the Solymians. When this test, too, and others afterwards, failed, Iobates gave up; he accepted Bellerophon as his son-in-law and made him his heir. More than one Lycian city in later times had a tribe named after Bellerophon.

The first appearance of Termessus in history is in connexion with Alexander's visit in 333 B.C.[1] Arrian's narrative includes an excellent description of the terrain. 'The site', he says, 'is very high and precipitous on all sides, and the passage by the road is difficult. The mountain descends from the city right to the road, and opposite to it is another hill equally abrupt. These hills form a kind of gate in the road, so that a small defence-force can easily render the passage impossible.' On Alexander's approach these slopes were occupied by the

[1] Above, p. 28.

Termessians in full force, and Alexander did not attempt to break through at once. Instead he pitched camp, suspecting that the enemy, on observing this, would not remain all night, but would prefer to retire to the city near by, leaving only a small force on guard. And so it turned out; the majority went back to their beds, and Alexander was easily able to rout the remainder. He thus passed the narrows and camped under the city, where he was joined by the envoys from Selge. These, though long-standing enemies of the Termessians, were not able, or did not try, to persuade him to destroy Termessus; at all events, the upshot was that he changed direction and made for Sagalassus. The scene of the encounter in the narrows must have been at or near the spot where the ruins of a handsome wall may now be seen crossing the valley, about half a mile east of the Yenice Kahve. Arrian makes no mention of any wall, and it is clear that none was standing in Alexander's time; the one now visible was built considerably later. There will be more to say of this wall below.

Fourteen years after these events, and four years after Alexander's death, there occurred an incident which is related for us in unusual detail by the historian Diodorus. At that time Antigonus, one of Alexander's generals and successors, was attempting to make himself master of Asia; he was opposed, among others, by a certain Alcetas, who was maintaining an army in the south and had won the friendship and support of the Pisidians. In 319 B.C. Antigonus turned upon him and defeated him utterly in a pitched battle. Alcetas himself escaped and took refuge with his Pisidian friends in Termessus; Antigonus followed and demanded his surrender. There was a division of opinion in the city; the elders were for the prudent course of giving Alcetas up, but the young fighting men were not prepared to consider this. The elders thereupon, failing to carry their point by persuasion, sent a secret embassy to Antigonus, urging him to make a pretence of a fighting withdrawal to a distance from the city; then, when the young warriors were thus drawn away and the coast clear, they would take Alcetas alive or dead and surrender him to Antigonus. The stratagem was approved and put into operation; the young Termessians swallowed the bait and Alcetas was left at the elders' mercy in the city. Unwilling, however, to fall alive into his enemies' hands, he put an end to his own life. The elders put his corpse on a stretcher, covered with a coarse garment, and succeeded in carrying it safely to Antigonus. When the young men returned and found what had happened their fury was extreme; so far from thanking their elders for saving the city, they even contemplated setting fire to it and taking to the mountains; but in the end they contented themselves with ravaging as much as they could of Antigonus' territory. Alcetas' body meanwhile had been shamefully treated by Antigonus; for three days he submitted it to all indignities, then, when it was beginning to decompose, he left it unburied and marched out of Pisidia. The young Termessians thereupon rescued it and gave it a splendid burial. This episode has a particular interest for the visitor to Termessus because it is not unlikely that the tomb they built for Alcetas may still be seen.[1]

During the third century little or nothing is heard of Termessus. From an interesting inscription found by the present writer at Araxa in Lycia we learn that at an uncertain date, perhaps about 200 B.C., the Termessians were at war with the Lycian League. It says a good deal for the citizens' warlike spirit that they could take on a confederation of some thirty cities. We do not know the result of the hostilities, but it appears that the Termessian territory was the scene of operations.

In 189 B.C. we find the bellicose tendencies of the Termessians again in evidence, when their attack on their neighbours of Isinda, some fifteen miles to the west, was thwarted by the intervention of the Roman consul Manlius Vulso.[2]

At some time earlier than this Termessus had, rather surprisingly, founded a colony. The site chosen was no less surprising, for it lay directly under the city of Oenoanda, about fifty miles to the west. Ancient writers refer to this colony as Termessus Minor, though in its inscriptions it calls itself Termessus-by-Oenoanda. It constitutes something of a puzzle. The site (identified at the modern Kemerarası) is feeble in the extreme; it comprises two low mounds strewn with ancient fragments, but never adequately fortified; it is

[1] Below, p. 134.   [2] Above, p. 30.

dominated by the mighty hill of Oenoanda and is militarily quite indefensible. The inscriptions, dating to the Roman period, mention a Council and Assembly and even refer to 'our splendid city', yet none of them were erected on the site; they are all found at Oenoanda. It is impossible to resist the conclusion that Termessus Minor, if it ever had any real independence, had lost it by imperial Roman times and had become absorbed into Oenoanda; the 'splendid city' is primarily Oenoanda. On the other hand it had its own constitution and even struck its own coins under the empire. The Termessians were never pacifists, and we hear much more of their enemies than of their friends; but they must have been on good terms with the Oenoandans at least, for Termessus Minor could never have been founded, or survived for a month, without their agreement.

In the course of the second century B.C. Termessus, that is Termessus Major, contracted a defensive alliance with the little Pisidian city of Adada. The fragmentary inscription which records this is of interest especially because it alludes to 'the democracy established in each of the cities'. Termessus had developed constitutionally since 319 B.C.; there is no hint in the story of Alcetas of any democratic institutions. Even at the later date we may suspect they were fairly primitive.

When Attalus II of Pergamum, about the middle of the second century, came south to subdue the resistance of Selge to his rule, Termessus, hereditary enemy of the Selgians, would be expected to support him. Though the historians say nothing, it appears that in fact they probably did so; at least, relations with the king must have been good, since he dedicated (and presumably paid for) the handsome portico which bordered the agora on the north-west.

Following the first Mithridatic War, in or about 70 B.C., the Roman people of their own volition made a treaty of friendship with Termessus, of which a considerable part is preserved. By this the Termessians are accepted as 'friends and allies' of the Roman people and are granted the right 'to use their own laws'; they were thus theoretically independent of the jurisdiction of the Roman governor of Cilicia. By a further provision no Roman soldiers are to be quartered in Termessus save by express order of the Senate, and the city is permitted to institute its own customs-dues by land and sea. This last is somewhat startling in its implication that Termessus had a harbour on the coast, and the surprise is increased when we read in another clause of 'such islands as the Termessians possess'. It is, in fact, out of the question that any such harbour or islands can have existed; Termessian territory certainly did not reach the coast, nor are there any islands in the neighbourhood save one uninhabited rock. The north-west corner of the gulf of Antalya was occupied by Olbia; and after the foundation of Attaleia any Termessian harbour on the coast would be even more effectively excluded. Evidently these clauses in the treaty are standard formulae, properly applicable only to coastal towns; Termessus was certainly not the only city with which similar treaties were made. Another clause refers to reparation for Termessian losses in the war against Mithridates; unless this, too, is a mere formula, we may conclude that Termessus was among the comparatively few who preferred to take the Roman part against the king.

Acceptance as the friend and ally of the Roman people was naturally a great thing for the Termessians, and they seem to have celebrated it by instituting a dating era beginning from, or soon after, 70 B.C. Coins of Termessus exist which appear to belong to the first century B.C. and are dated by the numbers from 1 to 32. The thirty-second year would then fall a little after 39 B.C., and in 36 Pisidia was given to Amyntas of Galatia,[1] who may well have put a stop to the series.

Under the empire, after Amyntas' death in 25 B.C., Termessus continued to enjoy her independence; coins of this period, down to the third century, carry the title 'Autonomous'. So proud indeed were the citizens of their qualified independence of the Roman rule that they asserted it in a most exceptional way—by never including on their coinage the image or titles of the Roman emperor. In later times the Byzantine lists record an episcopal see of Termessus, coupled frequently with Eudocias.[2] No church has yet been identified among the ruins, but this is not to say that none existed; excavation has yet to be undertaken.

[1] Above, p. 34.   [2] For Eudocias see above, p. 113.

The path up from Yenice Kahve (though not the new motor-
road) follows approximately the line of the ancient road,
called by the Termessians 'King Street'. This was constructed
in the second century A.D. from contributions of money by the
citizens; the subscription-list was published on stone and set up
near the market-square. At A it passes by a gate through the
outer fortification, a fine wall barring the valley, though its
middle part has now collapsed. On the inner east wall of the
gateway was inscribed the beginning of a dice-oracle, one of
the numerous specimens which are found in various parts of
Asia Minor.[1] These curious monuments to human credulity are
a feature of the middle and later years of the Roman empire, a
time when magic and all forms of superstition were in great
vogue. The oracular shrines of the old pagan gods were still
popular, but they were widely spaced and a visit to them
generally involved a considerable journey; to avoid this inconvenience the dice-oracles were introduced. They consisted
of a fixed set of prophecies, one for each possible throw of the
dice, inscribed sometimes on a wall of a temple, but often in
other public places as well. The dice used were called astragali,
the neck-bones of a sheep or other animal; there were four
sides on which they could rest (not six), counting respectively
one, three, four and six. Two and five could not be thrown.
Generally five dice were used, more rarely seven. The client
made his throw, then read from the inscribed list the appropriate 'response'. Five dice admit of fifty-six different
throws, and the various responses for these are known from
the surviving texts; for the most part they are the same in all
places, though variations do occur. They are couched in verse
—frequently very bad verse—in four or five lines: first a
heading naming the throw and its total count, together with
the name of a deity to whom it is supposed to belong, then a
verse describing the throw (though this is sometimes omitted),
followed by three verses giving the actual prophecy. There is a
remarkable sameness about the responses, and it seems that
the client was expected to ask only about the advisability of
some course of action; the god's advice is in effect confined to

---

[1] The inscribed blocks are now lying among the jumble of stones at
the roadside.

two alternatives: 'Go ahead', or 'Wait'. The client might save
himself trouble by tossing a coin. A typical example is:

> 44466   24   Cronos the Child-Eater
>
> Three fours and two sixes. This is the god's advice:
>
> Stay at home and go not elsewhere,
> Lest the destructive Beast and avenging Fury come upon
> you;
> For I see that the business is neither safe nor secure.

On the other hand:

> 66661   25   The Light-giving Moon-God.
>
> Four sixes, and the fifth a one. This is the meaning:
>
> Just as wolves overcome lambs, and mighty lions subdue
> Horned oxen, so shall you overcome all,
> And with the help of Hermes son of Zeus shall have all
> your desire.

That this dreadful rubbish should have had so wide a vogue
speaks poorly for the common sense of the ancients—though
the popularity nowadays of the horoscopes in the Sunday
newspapers no doubt runs it close. The oracle at the gate of
Termessus is of the less usual seven-dice type, which involves
120 responses, a total of 600 lines of writing. Only the first
few survive.

The principal ruins lie further up, above the second, or
inner, fortification-wall B. This wall is quite impressive, and
stands in part to its full height. To the left is the city-centre;
like the rest, it is much overgrown and would benefit from a
good clearing. The agora, or market-place (D), has some
unusual features. In the first place it is not strictly rectangular,
as the porticoes which border it are not at right-angles to one
another. It is artificially levelled and paved with stone slabs;
beneath the paving on the north-west side is a row of five
cisterns with circular mouths of varying sizes. But the most
remarkable feature is the heroum E on the south-west side.
Here, in a large outcrop of rock, a broad flight of steps leads
up to a platform some 20 feet square, at the back of which is a
semicircular bench. Above this is a wall, partly built of

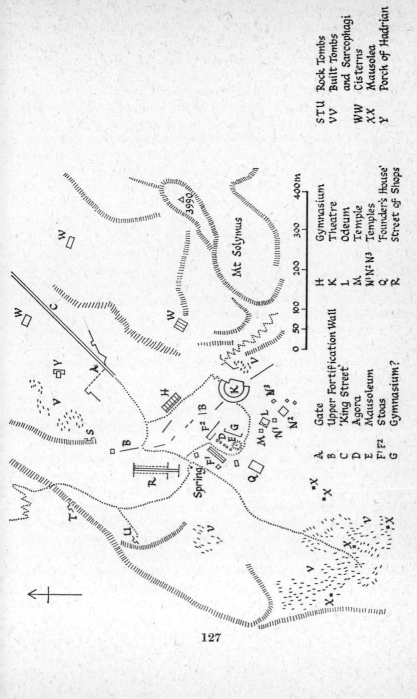

STU Rock Tombs
VV   Built Tombs
     and Sarcophagi
WW   Cisterns
XX   Mausolea
Y   Porch of Hadrian

Mt Solymus

A   Gate   H   Gymnasium
B   Upper Fortification Wall K   Theatre
C   'King Street'   L   Odeum
D   Agora   M   Temple
E   Mausoleum   N¹N²N³ Temples
F¹F² Stoas   Q   'Founder's House'
G   Gymnasium?   R   Street of Shops

0   50 100   200   300   400m

Fig. 24 Plan of Termessus

127

masonry, thick enough to contain a grave about 7 feet by 2
feet, originally covered by a separate lid which is now lost.
Whose tomb this may be is not known, as it carries no inscription and is not datable, but he must have been a man of
distinction, since burial in the market-place was an outstanding honour. The suggestion that we have here the tomb
of Alcetas, who was given distinguished burial by the Termessians,[1] does not seem to have been made; his tomb is con-
jecturally located elsewhere.[2] In the smoothed west face of the
rock are cut three large rounded niches; it is thought that these
may have been used for offerings to the hero. On the rough
sloping back of the rock are the names of two men carved in
large irregular letters; these are perhaps the proprietors of
other tombs let into the rock below; they have in any case no
connexion with the main tomb (Pl. 55).

On the north-west side the agora is bordered by the stoa, or
portico, of Attalus, presented to the city by Attalus II, king
of Pergamum (159–138 B.C.). It is identified by its dedicatory
inscription, of which fragments were found lying on the ground,
but at present little can be made of it.

A similar stoa borders the agora on the north-east; it was
built by a citizen of the name of Osbaras, of whom nothing
more is known. This building is at least 200 years later than the
stoa of Attalus, but it, too, offers little to the spectator.
Further to the north-east, at a lower level, is the large building
H, identified as a gymnasium. It is handsomely constructed
and much of it is standing, but the overgrowth makes inspection of it difficult.

Just to the east of the agora is the theatre, without doubt
the most attractive building at Termessus. It is not large, but
is well preserved and makes its appeal without the need of
excavation. The situation, too, is most impressive, with the
great rock of the mountain rising behind, and a steep gorge to
the right, down which a zigzag path leads to the Pamphylian
plain. The theatre is of the Greek type, with a cavea forming
more than a semicircle, and originally open passages (parodoi)
between it and the stage-building; of these the northern remains in its original form, the southern has undergone later

[1] Above, p. 122.   [2] Below, p. 134.

55   Termessus. Market-Place.

58   Termessus. Temple of Artemis.

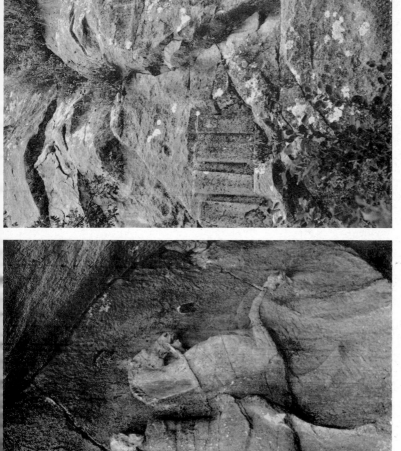

[*opposite*] 59 Termessus. Early Tomb, perhaps of Alcetas.

60 Termessus. Tomb of Alcetas (?). 61 Termessus. Tomb and Rock-Stelae.

62   Termessus. Built Tomb in the Necropolis.

[*opposite*]

63   Termessus. The Necropolis.

64   Termessus. Tower in the Wall across the valley.

67   Selge. The Theatre.

68   Selge. Stadium in foreground. Theatre behind.

[opposite]

69   Selge. Sarcophagus.

70   Phaselis. The Northern Harbour.

71   Phaselis. The Aqueduct.

[opposite]

72   The Coast north of Phaselis (Alexander's Route)

73   Phaselis. The Theatre.

75   Olympus. Temple Doorway.

74   Phaselis. Tombs on the Hillside.

76   Olympus. Tahtalı Dağ in the background.

77   Olympus. The 'Chimaera'.

alteration. There is one diazoma, with eight rows of seats above it and sixteen below; allowing 20 inches for each seat, it is calculated that there is room for 4,200 spectators.[1] The main entrance to the auditorium is by a door 8 feet wide in the middle of the back wall; this door was arched, and its keystone supported a statue of the youthful Heracles dedicated by the city. From this door a broad stairway leads down to the diazoma and so to the lower seats; but the upper seats were not accessible either from this stairway or from the diazoma, which has an uninterrupted back wall 6 feet high. They must have been reached by doors in the retaining wall above the level to which that is now preserved.

The stage-building consists simply of the stage and a long narrow room behind it. The back wall of the stage is rather roughly built of small blocks and contains five doors, the largest in the middle. Beneath the stage is a kind of basement, called the hyposcenium, which also has five doors into the orchestra; these are only 3 feet high and, as at Aspendus and elsewhere, were used to admit wild animals into the orchestra. In front of the back wall there stood as usual a row of columns, of which only the supports remain in place; those on either side of the central door had spiral fluting, the others are unfluted. The cavea, with its handsome regular ashlar masonry, dates from Hellenistic times. The stage-building is later, at least in its present form.

At a still later date a reconstruction was carried out at the south corner. An extension was made to the cavea, joining it to the stage-building and so providing some sixty or seventy extra seats; below the diazoma a 'Royal Box' or loggia was installed, and beneath this again a vaulted passage took the place of the earlier open parodos. These additional seats give a rather poor view of the stage, but would be useful when the

[1] This is no doubt an underestimate, as the allowance of 20 inches is certainly too large. In the Theatre of Dionysus at Athens the rows are marked with vertical lines 16 inches apart, which seem to indicate the individual seats. It is said that for seats without arms the London County Council regulations used to allow 18 inches, but that 16 was considered sufficient by theatre managers. A recent calculation even claims that 14 inches is adequate. The present writer, watching lawn tennis from an open stand, has found 16 inches enough, but not generous.

entertainment was in the orchestra rather than on the stage (as for wild beast shows and the like), or when the theatre was used for public assemblies (Pl. 56).

Close to the theatre, as at Sillyum and elsewhere, is a second and smaller theatre-like building or odeum. It is unusually well preserved, the walls standing over 30 feet high, but it is a good deal encumbered by vegetation, and the interior is largely filled with soil and débris. This is a building which would well repay clearing. The masonry is excellent and carefully dressed; it dates probably to the first century B.C. From the front the building seems to be divided into two storeys, but this is for the sake of appearance only; at the back the ground-level is much higher, and the interior is single-storeyed. The lower part of the walls on the outer face is plain, apart from two doors on the east front; the upper part is decorated with pilasters. In the east and south sides are windows, eleven in all. The interior faces of the walls are only roughly dressed, and were no doubt covered by some sort of veneer. In many places rims have been left uncut at the edges of the blocks; it was usual to leave such rims to protect the edges from damage during the process of construction, with the intention of shaving them away afterwards; but sometimes this was never done, either because the work was not properly finished or intentionally for decorative effect. Among the rubbish in the interior, parts of three rows of seats are, or were, discernible; they are curved, but form much less than a semicircle. In the back wall is an entrance for spectators; whether the two doors on the east were used by spectators or actors or both is not clear in the present condition of the building. The windows suggest that the whole building was roofed, but how the width of nearly 80 feet was spanned does not appear (Pl. 57).

On the upper part of the north wall of the odeum, between the pilasters, are cut inscriptions recording the names of victors in the games; they are thought to have been placed in this position in order to be visible from the upper gymnasium G. At present they are not visible at all except in a favourable light; but originally the letters would have been painted red. The events mentioned comprise horse-races, foot-races, races in armour, and wrestling. Numerous inscriptions at Termessus honour the victors in a variety of athletic contests, mostly instituted at the expense of rich citizens; the overwhelming majority record victories in wrestling, which was evidently something of a speciality among the Termessians. Wrestling and foot-races normally took place in the stadium, horse-racing in the hippodrome; neither of these buildings has been identified at Termessus.

Directly behind the odeum is a small temple (M), whose walls, beautifully built and finished, still stand 17 feet high. It is thought to be connected with the worship of Solymian Zeus, though not his principal temple, for which it appears too modest. Nothing but the walls remains, except for a bench across the back wall which held statues. The main temple of Solymian Zeus was certainly in this neighbourhood, where numerous remnants associated with him have been found, but nothing of it seems to survive above ground.

Just to the south of the odeum is another small temple (N[1]), also well preserved, but much encumbered by over-growth. The door is standing complete, with an inscription recording that the temple and cult-statue were constructed at her own expense and dedicated to Artemis by one Aurelia Armasta, with her husband's help, while the decoration and six silver images were presented by her mother. Bases on either side of the door carried statues, now lost, of her uncles (Pl. 58). The building belongs probably to the first half of the third century A.D.; at this date it is obviously unlikely to be the first temple of Artemis at Termessus, and, in fact, a predecessor is identifiable with considerable probability. This is the temple just across the way (N[2]), of which only the foundations now survive; from the architectural fragments lying around it is clear that it was in the Ionic order, with six columns at front and back and eleven at the sides. Among the ruins were found a dedication to Artemis and two reliefs showing the sacrifice of Iphigenia, an event in which Artemis played a leading part.

From N[2] a stairway leads down on the north to a terrace cut in the hillside; on this are the ruins of yet another small temple (N[3]). It stands on a high substructure, or podium, with a flight of steps on the west. On the blocks of the walls at the south-east corner may be seen mason's marks in the form of letters of the alphabet, indicating the position to be occupied by each block. It is not known to what deity this temple belonged; the entrance on the west suggests a hero or demigod, for the temples of the gods were normally entered from the east.[1]

Another well-preserved building is that known as the Founder's House (Q). It appears indeed to be a private house of the Roman type, but on a very splendid scale. The front door, on the west, stands not less than 18 feet high; on its left jamb is an inscription, roughly cut and legible only in a favourable light,[2] complimenting a certain Besas, founder of the city. The word 'founder', however, does not mean what it seems to mean; it must be understood in the same sense as the Roman 'founders' of Perge.[3] We may suppose (if we wish) that Besas was the owner of the house, and that the inscription was cut by some admirer or client with or without his permission. To the left of the door was a window, above which was a carving showing a perching bird and two humps in the form of half an egg. This device caught the attention of Lieutenant Spratt in 1842; he conjectured that it might be connected with some sort of divination by birds. In support of this suggestion he pointed to a 'smaller edifice of ancient structure communicating with it, having in the centre three erect projections of rock with steps carved on their sides'. (The present writer has not seen these.) The window has now fallen, and Spratt's carving is not to be seen; on the other hand, lying among the débris is another similar block with a carving of a bird with spread wings. The two designs are shown in the accompanying sketches. But Spratt's interpretation has not been taken up by subsequent investigators. Inside the door is a vestibule, with a bench against each wall, leading through by a second door 10 feet high to the atrium or main hall of the house. In the centre is the impluvium, or rain-water basin, surrounded by columns of which only two stumps remain in place. The whole of this building is thickly overgrown.

In the western part of the city, on the other side of the main

[1] There are, however, exceptions; see *Aegean Turkey*, pp. 250, 267.
[2] The present writer has never been able to find it.
[3] Above, p. 53.

street, the principal feature is a road (R) running north and south, bordered on each side by porticoes and shops. There were at least forty-seven columns on either side, and in front of each (and sometimes between them) stood a statue; not one of the statues survives, only the inscribed bases. Of these more than half commemorate victories in the games, almost exclusively in the wrestling; others honour priests, magistrates and other public officials. Here again investigation is rendered difficult by the dense jungle.

FIG. 25a, b Termessus. Carved blocks at the 'Founder's House'

An important feature of the site, for the ancients as for the modern visitor, is the spring of excellent water just to the right of the path on the way up. It lies down in a hole, and a cup or other vessel is useful. From here a side-path leads up to the north and west, where a number of interesting rock-tombs are to be seen; but they are not easy to find without a guide. At S is a handsome group of five tombs; the three lower are in the form of semicircular niches (called arcosolia) and are later than the other two. Higher up to the west, at T, is another tomb whose general appearance recalls the rock-tombs of Lycia. Its form is modelled on that of a wooden house, with a façade in two parts and the round beam-ends of the roof above. On the other hand the Ionic pillars, the entablature and the pediment are Greek, though the ornament at the summit (the acroterium) is a further Lycian feature. These rock-tombs are the earliest at Termessus, but none of them carries any inscription.

The most interesting of all is at U, a tomb quite unlike anything else on the site—or indeed elsewhere in the present writer's experience. Unfortunately it has suffered a good deal recently from the attentions of treasure-seekers. Set in an angle of the vertical rock-face is a stone bench, above which is a ledge about 2 feet 6 inches wide; in this was cut the actual grave, but this part is now broken away. Above is a trellis-work between columns, with a pediment above which is now mostly lost. This was perhaps intended to suggest a kind of baldachin or canopy over the grave. At the top is a spread-eagle holding a snake in his claws (Pl. 59).

To right and left of the main tomb are various reliefs and cuttings in the rock. Immediately to the right is a square projection with a lion's head (now smashed) on the front and a large square sinking in its upper surface; to the right of this is a small figure of Hermes (smashed), and to the right again a figure of Aphrodite; beyond this is a circular excavation 16 inches deep with a lion's head on a panel in front. To the left of the tomb, on the projecting rock-wall, is a fine relief (Pl. 60) showing a mounted warrior (the face smashed); lower down on the right is a suit of armour—a helmet (smashed), a pair of greaves, and a round shield (smashed) with a sword set diagonally across it. Beside the shield some have thought to discern traces of an inscription, but this, if it exists, is utterly illegible. Immediately to the left of the tomb is yet another deep sinking some 2 feet square; it was originally provided with a lid, and was perhaps a receptacle for the bones or ashes of the dead. The other sinkings had no lid, and their purpose is not really known, unless it be to hold water.

This tomb, unique at Termessus and certainly among the earliest, is not unlikely to be that of Alexander's general Alcetas. The circumstances of his death at Termessus were related above, and he is said to have been given 'splendid' burial. Under Alexander he had served as an infantry general, but it appears from Diodorus' narrative that in his last battle against Antigonus he fought on horseback; this would explain the relief showing at the same time a mounted warrior and a foot-soldier's armour. It is noteworthy that the warrior here wears armour identical with that worn by Alexander in the famous mosaic, now at Naples, depicting the battle of Issus; and in general the style of the tomb and the relief is perfectly consistent with a date at the end of the fourth century. Above the path leading up to this tomb from the spring is the group shown on Pl. 60.

The great mass of the tombs in the upper part of the city to the south-west is considerably later than the rock-tombs, and dates in general to the first three centuries A.D. Buried among the woods, they are very picturesque, and many of them are still well preserved (Pl. 62, 63). The majority consist of a sarcophagus on a base, more or less elaborately worked and decorated, but some are quite impressive structures of temple-form or similar shape, containing one or more sarcophagi. Most of the tombs carry an inscription (650 have been read and published) naming the owner and any other persons whom he permits to be buried with him; this is followed generally, though not always, by specific penalties for any violation of the tomb. The penalties take the form of a fine, often accompanied by a curse or a threat of prosecution for tomb-robbery or impiety. The fines are payable most often to Solymian Zeus, frequently also to the imperial chest or the city treasury, in one case to the shrine of the Healer Achilles; they vary in amount from 300 to 100,000 denarii, the latter equal to several thousand pounds sterling. Provision is often made for the informer to receive a half or a third of the money. How the amounts were determined is not known; every man would no doubt wish his grave to be protected by as high a penalty as possible, and it may be that he paid to the body named a fixed proportion of the fine he desired to be imposed. These threats and penalties were not always effective, at least not in perpetuity; in the case of the highest fine of all, 100,000 denarii, the original sarcophagus has later been moved aside and two others installed.

About half a mile east of the Yenice Kahve, and a little to

the west of the new Termessus road, the present main road, which is also the ancient, is crossed by a fine fortification-wall still well preserved in part. It is in good ashlar masonry, with ten towers and a gate close beside the present highway. It is dated to the second century B.C. One of the towers, a little to the south of the road, is in particularly good condition, with a door on the uphill side level with the ground (Pl. 64). This wall has attracted the attention of all travellers in modern times and has caused much perplexity, for it seems to face the wrong way. The towers are on its west side, so that it is apparently directed against an army advancing from that quarter, in which case it would halt an enemy only after he had passed the foot of Termessus. It has accordingly been thought that the wall cannot be the work of the Termessians at all, but must have been built by their Pamphylian enemies to keep them in their mountain fastnesses and prevent them from raiding the plain. This was the opinion of Lieutenant Spratt, who first saw the wall, and it is shared by Freya Stark and others. In the present writer's view this explanation is altogether improbable. It is not really credible that the Termessians should ever have permitted the wall to be built; or, if they were unable to prevent it, that it could have been effectively manned for any length of time against their opposition. Nor in any case could it serve its purpose; they had other ways of reaching the plain. We must surely accept that the Termessians were the builders.

The wall has another peculiarity: it does not effectively bar the valley. On the north side of the road it runs up a more or less isolated hill, beyond which is the bed of the stream which comes down from the heights on the west into the Pamphylian plain, but this the wall does not cross; it ends on the south slope of the hill. The credit for noticing this weakness belongs to Freya Stark, though she does not draw any conclusion from it. A solution of the problem may, however, be possible. It has long seemed to the writer that the wall, though unquestionably a military fortification, was never primarily intended as a defence wall. The defences of Termessus lie much higher up, and can hardly be considered inadequate. More likely, surely, the wall was built by the Termessians to give them control over all passage through the defile, and the power to levy toll

on all who wished to pass that way. The escape route by the
stream could be used at a pinch by infantry or pedestrians, if
they knew of it, but was, of course, very easily defensible even
without a wall. The position of the wall was chosen simply as
being the most easily controllable point in the valley. Even
when it was not there, Arrian observes that a small garrison
could make the road impassable. Against an army coming
from the east the wall would be somewhat less effective; but
merchants and other travellers would be a rich source of
profit. It may well be that this wall was an important reason
for the great prosperity of Termessus in the centuries after it
was built.

CHAPTER TEN

*

Selge

FOR THE ENTERPRISING traveller Selge offers a most attractive excursion with a charm all its own. The site is remote, far more so than Termessus, and high up in the hills; it is seldom visited. However, a forestry road has recently been constructed leading directly to the site, and it is now possible to do the return journey by jeep in a single day from Manavgat or even from Antalya. But for a thorough exploration it is better to spend a night in the village. And the effort is abundantly rewarded; it is delightful to find the extensive ruins of a large city in so secluded a place, but no less so to make the acquaintance of its present inhabitants. Some ancient grammarians derived the Greek word *aselges*, 'rude' or 'licentious', from the name of the city; since the prefix *a*- can have either a negative or an intensive meaning, the word could be interpreted as 'unlike the men of Selge' or 'very like the men of Selge' according to preference. If the modern villagers preserve anything of the character of their ancient predecessors, there can be no hesitation; the present writer has never anywhere, even in the hospitable land of Turkey, been more charmingly received and entertained.

Selge preserves its ancient name in the form Zerk.[1] The village is poor, and in a bad season desperately so; yet the soil is naturally good, and Strabo speaks highly of its fertility, with vines and olives and abundant pasture; the population, he says, rose at one time to 20,000. As regards the olives at least he must be alluding to some part of Selgian territory less elevated than the city itself, whose altitude is little short of 900 metres, whereas olives do not normally grow much above 2,000 feet, and in fact none grow at Zerk today. But shortage

[1] To be carefully distinguished from the town of Serik on the Antalya highroad.

of water is the trouble nowadays, and when the rainfall is
meagre there is real hardship; this was the case at the time of
the writer's visit in 1951, and again when Freya Stark was there
a few years later. Visitors can therefore be a serious burden to
the villagers (though they will be none the less courteously
welcomed for that) and the traveller who intends to stay overnight should, for their sake and his own, take provisions with
him. The ancient city was supplied by an aqueduct leading
from the hills above; the earthenware pipes of its water-system
may be seen in many parts of the ruins.

The jeep road from Taşağıl follows the valley of the Eurymedon to the *nahiye* of Beşkonak. At several points it is
crossed by streams which in winter or after rain may well be
impassable to any form of motor transport. Over the largest,
the Sağırın Çayı, there is a rickety-looking wooden bridge
which the writer has not put to the test. Beyond Beşkonak
the road continues up the river for another three miles or so to
a most attractive and excellently preserved Roman bridge
(Pl. 65); this has a single arch and is as sound today as when
it was built. Crossing by this, the traveller begins a climb of
over 2,000 feet. The track is steep at first, following roughly
the course of the ancient road, stretches of whose paving still
survive in several places (Pl. 66). Towards the top of the ascent
the rock-formations are very curious, making pillars, gateways
and corridors, all apparently natural; and some two miles
from the village of Zerk is a remarkable ancient well with a
double shaft in the form of a figure 8. All of these, however, lie
off the line of the new road.

According to the ancient tradition Selge was first founded
by Calchas and afterwards resettled by Spartans. It is surprising to find the 'mixed multitude' of early settlers making
their way so far up into the mountains, and it may be that this
claim is no more than a reflection of the Selgians' desire to be
associated with the cities of the plain; though generally reckoned a Pisidian city, Selge was constantly at enmity with her
Pisidian neighbours and looked for preference to the south.
So in the fifth century B.C., and later, she struck silver coins
virtually indistinguishable from those of Aspendus, showing
on the obverse a pair of wrestlers and on the reverse a slinger.

There seems to have been a monetary convention between the two cities. These early coins carry the city's name in the form Stlegiys or Estlegiys, recalling the early name of Aspendus, Estwediiys. These names are quite un-Greek and must go back to very ancient times.

Strabo, emphasising the wild and precipitous nature of the country, and the highly civilised government of the city, observes that Selge never at any time until the Roman domination came under the power of others, but cultivated her own land in security and even strove with the Hellenistic kings for the possession of 'the land below in Pamphylia'. No details are given, but her interest in the coastal plain is evident.

When Alexander arrived in 333 B.C. the Selgians were among the few that offered him voluntary friendship. Their motive in doing so is not obvious; Alexander had certainly never any designs upon their remote city, and indeed was in process of quitting the country when they sent their ambassadors to him near Termessus.[1] Arrian suggests that they acted out of hostility to the Termessians, as if willing to help him in his contemplated attack; but in fact the immediate sequel to their embassy was that Alexander abandoned Termessus and marched to the north. It may be that they did indeed come with the idea of joining the attack on Termessus, but finding that Alexander was unenthusiastic for a long siege earned his gratitude in another way by suggesting to him a better route to Phrygia by way of Sagalassus. For the Selgians were no more amicably disposed towards the Sagalassians than towards the Termessians.

About the year 220 B.C. occurred the principal appearance of the Selgians in history. Not that the incident was important in itself or that it had any lasting consequences, but the story is told by Polybius in considerable detail and gives an interesting picture of the times. The Selgians were besieging their neighbours of Pednelissus,[2] and these, finding themselves in danger,

---

[1] Above, p. 28.
[2] The site of this city is not known with certainty. It has been proposed to identify it with the Hellenistic site above Kozan, some twenty-two miles north-north-east of Perge and eleven miles due west of Selge. To the present writer this identification seems highly probable. Strabo says merely that Pednelissus is 'above Aspendus'.

applied to Achaeus for help.[1] Achaeus responded by sending
his general Garsyeris with a force of 6,000 men to raise the
siege. The Selgians thereupon occupied the passes to prevent
his advance. There followed some skirmishing which we cannot
clearly understand, as the places named are all unidentified;[2]
the upshot was that the Selgians were dislodged by a trick, and
Garsyeris, after collecting another 12,000 men from Etenna
and Aspendus in Pamphylia, arrived before Pednelissus,
expecting to raise the siege without difficulty. But the Selgians
gave no ground, and he contented himself with encamping a
little way off and sending provisions to the besieged; these,
however, were intercepted by the Selgians, who were thereby
encouraged to conceive the idea of besieging not only the city
but Garsyeris' encampment into the bargain. In this they
overreached themselves and were defeated with heavy losses;
they abandoned the siege and retired to their own city, closely
followed by Garsyeris. The boot was now on the other leg, and
fearing for their own safety they decided to send an ambassador to treat for peace, choosing for the purpose a citizen
named Logbasis, who had in the past been intimate with
Achaeus and seemed a likely man to obtain good terms. He,
however, shamefully belied this trust, and proposed to Garsyeris that Achaeus himself should be urged to come, promising
to betray the city to him. Garsyeris agreed, and spun out the
negotiations till Achaeus should arrive, which in due course he
did. Meanwhile a good deal of fraternisation had taken place,
and the Selgians were in high hopes of a favourable settlement;
they accordingly called an assembly to discuss what terms they
should ask. This was Logbasis' opportunity; giving the signal
to the enemy, he armed himself and his sons and followers and
awaited the outcome in his house. Achaeus promptly advanced
with half his force against the city gates, leaving Garsyeris to
attack the so-called Kesbedion.[3] It happened, however, that a
goatherd observed these proceedings and gave the alarm. The
Selgians in this crisis did not fail their reputation for bravery;

[1] Above, p. 29.
[2] They are Climax, Saporda and Cretopolis, none of which has been
satisfactorily located.
[3] Below, pp. 143, 145.

breaking up the assembly, they rushed to arms and hurriedly occupied the Kesbedion, while a crowd ran to the house of Logbasis and slaughtered all its occupants. Garsyeris, seeing that he was too late, gave up and withdrew, and Achaeus' assault on the gate was no more successful; the Selgians made a sortie, killed 700 of Achaeus' men and drove off the attack. In this way, says Polybius, they saved their city and their freedom and did not disgrace their kinship with the Spartans. Nevertheless, feeling that honour was satisfied, and fearful of further treachery from within, they made their peace with Achaeus on the terms that they should pay forthwith a sum of 400 talents (close on half a million sterling) and another 300 later, and should surrender their Pednelissian prisoners.

This episode virtually completes the recorded history of Selge. When the Romans first arrived the Selgians came to an arrangement with them that enabled them to keep their territory and their independence; later they were included in the lands assigned to Amyntas,[1] and by the time of the early empire they were completely incorporated in the Roman dominions. Strabo calls them 'the most noteworthy of the Pisidians'; their city was prosperous, and its citizens travelled widely, being frequently met with in other parts of Asia Minor; it issued an abundant coinage down to the latter part of the third century A.D. Apart from vines and olives, the Selgian territory produced an iris, from which a highly esteemed unguent was made and used for massage, and above all the storax plant, which appears commonly on the coins. Strabo describes this as a small tree infested with a kind of woodworm that bores through the stem, extruding a wood-dust which collects in a heap at the foot of the tree; this is followed by a rapidly congealing resinous liquid like gum, which trickles down the stem and mixes with the dust and earth at the foot; such of it, however, as congeals on the stem remains pure. This resin, says Strabo, 'is used as incense by the superstitious'; the impure is more fragrant than the pure, but in other respects inferior. Storax-gum is no longer used commercially today.

The extent of the ruins reveals clearly enough the im-

[1] Above, p. 34.

portance of the city, at least under the Roman empire; but for all her size and prosperity she never produced a really distinguished man. The best known of her citizens remains the traitor Logbasis.

The ruins of Selge lie on and around three separate hills, of which the highest, on the west, is identified with the Kesbedion named by Polybius. The whole was enclosed by a wall, over two miles long, of which the line can be made out and some stretches are reasonably well preserved. The most considerable piece is on the south-west (AB on the plan), but in its present condition belongs to a later repair; it has towers at intervals of 100 yards or so. At A is a gate which is probably that attacked by Achaeus, and at B is a larger tower of at least two storeys. Just inside the gate A is the small building N, with three rooms of good masonry; this is thought to have been possibly a customs-house.

From Zerk the visitor begins his tour of inspection most naturally with the theatre C. This is of above average size, the lower part cut out of the rocky hillside, the upper part constructed of masonry. The cavea is more than a semicircle, as in Greek theatres in general, but is joined to the stage-building in the Roman fashion—evidently in consequence of later alterations. There is a single diazoma, with thirty rows of seats below it and fifteen above; these are divided vertically by stairways, twelve in number both above and below the diazoma. More usually the number of stairways is doubled in the upper part of the theatre. At the end of the cavea is a parapet curiously equipped with small windows and cuttings of which the purpose is obscure (Pl. 67).

Four entrances lead from outside to the diazoma, affording access to the lower rows of seats and apparently also to the upper rows, but in the present condition of the theatre the exact arrangement is not easy to make out.

The stage-building is a jumble of collapsed masonry, but its general form can be discerned. Its inner wall, facing the auditorium, contained the usual five doors giving access to the stage, but only three of these are now visible. Its outer or back wall has two doors visible, with presumably a third in the middle now buried, and a window at each end. In the short wall at the west end is a small arched door and another, much larger, leading through into the orchestra. On the adjoining wall is a large panel for an inscription that was never written.

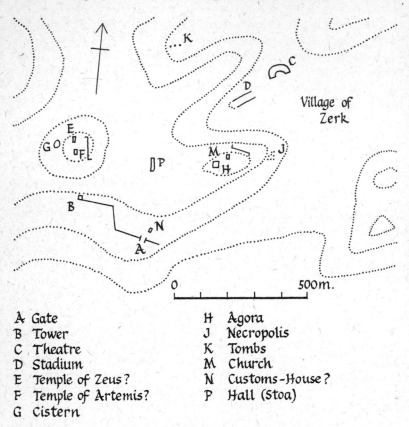

A Gate
B Tower
C Theatre
D Stadium
E Temple of Zeus?
F Temple of Artemis?
G Cistern

H Agora
J Necropolis
K Tombs
M Church
N Customs-House?
P Hall (Stoa)

FIG. 26 Plan of Selge

The stadium, just below the theatre on the south-west, is only indifferently preserved. It had seats on either side, those on the north resting on the slope of the hill, those on the south on a vaulted gallery of which a small part survives. The preserved length is somewhat less than a stade, the width something over thirty yards. Normally, of course, the length should be rather over a stade, to allow space for the stadium race; but in fact considerably shorter stadia—or at least stadium-like structures—are not uncommonly found,[1] though they can hardly have been used for full-scale games. At Selge a number of inscriptions have been found recording victories in the games held in the stadium; for the most part these games were open only to citizens of Selge, but every fourth year a more brilliant festival was held. Even this, however, was of no great repute and is not otherwise heard of. Nevertheless we should expect a full-size stadium at Selge, and it is likely that it was, in fact, longer than it is now (Pl. 68).

The identification of the western hill with the Kesbedion is conjectural and unsupported by any actual evidence. We have, in fact, no ancient information about the city itself beyond what Polybius says, and we are dependent on the inscriptions found on the surface; for so extensive a city these are comparatively few and uninformative. This hill is, however, the most impressive of the three and carries the two principal temples.

Of these the northern, E, is thought to be the temple of Zeus, the main sanctuary of the city, though this again is unproved. The other, F, is perhaps that of Artemis; the evidence for this is the occurrence of a priestess of Artemis in an inscription found close by, but this, too, is of course inconclusive. Both these temples now lie in ruins; neither here nor elsewhere on the site has any excavation been done.

At the back of this hill, at G, is a large round tank or cistern some 70 feet in diameter and still some 25 feet deep. It was fed not only by rain-water but by a channel leading from the north-west; high in the hills in that direction there are still some remains of a handsome aqueduct similar to that which served Side.

On the level ground between this hill and the third or southern hill, at P, stood a long hall or stoa some 120 yards in length; at its southern end there stands a very tall pillar on which are cut two inscriptions.

On the third hill, at H, is the agora or market-place. This is a paved area some 50 yards square, open on the south, with

[1] For example, at Arycanda, Theangela, Myndus and Iasus.

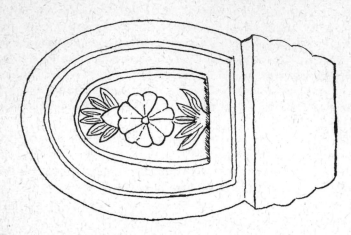

FIG. 28 Carved stone at Selge

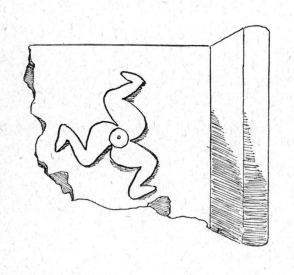

FIG. 27 Carved stone at Selge

146

buildings on the other three sides. Close by, at M, the ruins of
a church remind us that Selge was later the seat of a bishop,
ranking next after Side and before Aspendus.

The main group of tombs is at J, but they have suffered
considerable damage in recent years. The sarcophagi are
distinctive in their decoration (Pl. 69); a curious device re-
curring more than once is that of two small circles in the
upper part of a larger circle, giving something of the appearance of a pair of eyes in a face. On the slope beyond the
northern hill, at K, are three large built tombs, only partially
preserved.

Quite apart from the monuments mentioned above, the
visitor will see numberless other cut blocks, reliefs (Figs. 27,
28), architectural members and fragmentary buildings, but for
the most part the purposes of these cannot at present be
determined.

PART FOUR

Lycia

*

CHAPTER ELEVEN

Phaselis

AMONG THE outstanding memories which the traveller brings away from his first visit to Antalya must surely be the view of the Lycian mountains across the bay. Rising from the sea in a jumbled succession of fairy-tale peaks to a height of just over 10,000 feet, they make a formidable introduction to the Land of Tombs. Lycia is indeed a hard country. It contains two fertile regions in the lower valleys of the Esen and Alâkır rivers, the latter famous for the oranges of Finike, the former for the recently excavated city of Xanthus; for the rest it is dry, stony and mountainous, largely roadless and waterless. By the shore the summer heat is oppressive, and in July most of the villages are more or less deserted in favour of the *yaylas*, or summer quarters, high up in the hills. This, however, is not the place to tell of the Lycian people or of the fascinating ruins of their cities; two places only must suffice, Phaselis and Olympus—and these not originally Lycian at all, for in early times the boundaries of Lycia did not extend eastwards of the Alâkır valley. No inscriptions in the Lycian language, nor any of the characteristic types of Lycian tomb, are found on the east coast. In recent years chrome mines were worked for a time in the neighbourhood of Olympus, with a station on the shore at Çıralı, but these have now been abandoned as unprofitable. The road from Antalya is fair as far as Kemer, after that passable for a jeep but very rough. Caiques do the journey to Phaselis in about five hours. In summer the sea is normally calm in the morning, but tends to get up with the wind in the afternoon.

Of the two cities in question Phaselis was in antiquity by far the more distinguished, and has quite a history of its own. It was founded by colonists from Rhodes; their leader's name was Lacius, and the date is given precisely as 690 B.C. The tradition is, however, a little confused; some said that Lacius was not a Rhodian but an Argive, and was sent with a party of men by Mopsus to found Phaselis. One account says even that the city was founded by Mopsus himself. Mopsus lived, of course, long before 690 B.C., so that if this tradition has any basis in fact the Rhodian settlement must have been a refoundation; this would help to explain why Phaselis was regarded in early times as a Pamphylian city. But we shall probably do best to leave Mopsus out of the reckoning and regard Phaselis as a straightforward Rhodian colony. Herodotus in the fifth century groups it with Rhodes in a list of Dorian states, and the early inscriptions, down to 300 B.C., are written in the special Rhodian variety of the Doric dialect.

The foundation legend said that when Lacius and his party arrived they found the land on which they desired to build their city in the possession of a shepherd called Cylabras, and offered to buy it from him for a quantity either of corn or of dried fish; money had at that time not been invented. Cylabras chose the fish; and in consequence, even down to late times, it was the custom at Phaselis to offer sacrifice of dried fish, and the expression 'a Phaselitan sacrifice' became proverbial for a cheap offering.

The site is well placed for a trading-station on the route from Greece to Syria and Palestine, and may indeed have been used in this capacity, before the Rhodians came, by the Phoenicians, the great traders of early antiquity; the name Phaselis has been explained as Semitic, meaning 'God saves'. In Greek, on the other hand, *phaselos* means the garavance or chickpea, and the city's name was popularly associated with this.

However this may be, the Phaselitans were great traders from the start. When Amasis, king of Egypt in the early sixth century, permitted the Greeks to build the city of Naucratis in the Delta for purposes of commerce, nine cities of Asia Minor joined in founding the principal sanctuary, the Hellenium; of these Phaselis was one, and the only one from the south coast. Phaselitan coins, from the fifth century onwards, commonly show on one side the prow of a ship and on the other the stern.

When the Persians overran Asia Minor in the middle of the sixth century, Phaselis came under their power with the rest; and the famous Greek victories at Marathon, Salamis and Plataea, which freed the cities of the west coast from the Persian grip, did not affect their hold on the south. Liberation came later, in 469, with the expedition of the Athenian general Cimon;[1] and like so many other cities Phaselis was liberated against her will. Plutarch tells the story in his Life of Cimon: 'On arriving at Phaselis he found that the citizens, though Greeks, received him ill and were not ready to defect from the Great King; he therefore began to ravage their territory and attack the walls. However, the Chians who were sailing with him, being friends of long standing with the Phaselitans, did their best to restrain him, and at the same time shot leaflets, attached to arrows, over the walls to tell the inhabitants what was happening. Finally they brought the parties to terms, the Phaselitans agreeing to pay ten talents and accompany Cimon on his campaign against the barbarians.'

The result of this campaign was that Phaselis became a member of the Athenian maritime confederacy, known as the Delian League.[2] She was assessed for tribute at a sum varying from three to six talents, and this she regularly paid. It is a measure of her importance at that time that six talents was the amount normally paid by Ephesus.

When the Persian rule was restored in Asia Minor in the fourth century, a certain Carian by the name of Mausolus was appointed satrap of Caria. Mausolus was an able man and ambitious, and he made himself virtually independent of Persia, extending his sway not only over Caria but over Lycia also. The Lycians, always jealous of their freedom, resisted under their dynast Pericles, and it appears that Phaselis aided Mausolus against them. Polyaenus, in his book of Stratagems, tells how a certain Charimenes of Miletus took refuge from this Pericles in Phaselis; as the dynast's ships were blockading the sea route, he disguised himself in a wig and escaped on foot through Pericles' territory. In 1874 there was found in Antalya a considerable fragment of a treaty between Mausolus and Phaselis, engraved on stone; it concerns among other things the payment

---

[1] Above, pp. 25–6. [2] Above, p. 25.

of judicial debts on either side, and the independent status of the city is shown by the fact that the parties sign as equals.

Alexander arrived at Phaselis in the early months of 333 B.C. The Phaselitans had already sent envoys to offer him their friendship and a golden crown, and surrendered their city to him. Alexander stayed in the city for some while, and lent the aid of his troops to suppress a neighbouring stronghold of the Pisidians, who were using it to raid the Phaselitan farm-lands. After Phaselis his next destination was Perge, but there was no regular road, only a difficult and roundabout route over the mountains. It was, however, possible, when the wind was from the north, to make one's way along the shore; at other times the sea washed the foot of the mountains, which here descend right to the shore, leaving no room to pass. As a south wind was blowing at the time, Alexander sent a part of his army by the long route over the hills; suddenly, however, by a divine providence as he was convinced, the wind changed to the north, and he himself with the rest of his men made his way easily and quickly along the beach.

This at least is Arrian's account. Strabo, however, making no mention of the winds, says merely that the passage along the shore is usable in calm weather but not when the sea is up, and that Alexander, happening on rough weather, started off without waiting for it to change, preferring to trust to luck, so that the men marched all day with the water up to their waists. It is not today, and probably never was, possible to walk all the way from Phaselis to the Pamphylian plain along the shore. The greater part of the way is indeed easy: there is a broad sandy beach: but in two places the cliffs descend into deepish water, and in normal conditions at least it is necessary to cross the neck of the promontory—in one case a considerable detour (Pl. 72). Local fishermen with whom the present writer spoke said that the wind makes no appreciable difference to the level of the sea, but a *north* wind tends to produce rougher water. They were not prepared to deny that under very favourable conditions it *might* be possible to walk round the headlands with the water up to chest height; but reliable information is hardly to be had, as no one nowadays ever considers doing such a thing. Since the sea-level was certainly

higher in Alexander's time than it is today,[1] the present sandy
beach may well not have existed, and we may picture the
Macedonians marching as Strabo describes, with at least two
digressions overland which he does not mention.[2]

In the troubled times that followed Alexander's death
Phaselis came early into the possession of the kings of Egypt.
At first Antigonus, one of the ablest of Alexander's generals,
attempted to control the west of Asia Minor, and had garrisons
in some at least of the Lycian cities; but in 309 B.C. Ptolemy I
ejected these by force. Phaselis resisted in Antigonus' interest,
but fell to a siege; Xanthus, the capital city of Lycia, was taken
by storm, and the country remained a Ptolemaic possession
down to the end of the third century. The Egyptian control
was, however, very weak, and in 197 B.C. Antiochus III of
Syria had no difficulty in overrunning Lycia in addition to
Cilicia and Pamphylia. No mention of Phaselis or Olympus is
made in this campaign, but they must have fallen with the
rest. Antiochus' rule was brief; defeated by the Romans at
Magnesia in 190 he was expelled from these parts and Lycia
was given to the Rhodians, who had been good allies of the
Romans during the war. The Lycians, with their passionate
love of freedom, bitterly resented and violently resisted the
Rhodian rule, and in 167 B.C. the Roman Senate was persuaded
to declare Lycia free.

With their desire for freedom the Lycian cities combined a
capacity for co-operation which was unusual in classical
Greek times. From quite an early date there had existed some
kind of confederation, and from 167 B.C. onwards we find a
fully developed Lycian League, with a constitution which won
the admiration of the ancients and induced the Romans to
leave Lycia free longer than any other part of Asia Minor.
In this League Phaselis was included, and struck coins in the
second century B.C. of the federal type common to all the
Lycian cities. Throughout all the centuries hitherto Phaselis
had not been reckoned Lycian at all, but was regarded as
attached to Pamphylia; it is likely that her transference to
Lycia was due to the Rhodian occupation—for Phaselis was a

---

[1] Below, pp. 171, 173.
[2] See also Freya Stark, *Alexander's Path*, pp. 85–87.

Rhodian foundation, and it would be natural to include her with her western neighbours when these became a possession of Rhodes. What happened after the Rhodians left in 167 is not very clear. The coins just mentioned suggest that she continued to be attached to Lycia, but about 100 B.C. we learn that she was not a Lycian city but had her own independent constitution. The reason for this separation is not known, but it certainly continued for some time after 100 B.C. Early in the first century Phaselis, together with her neighbour Olympus and much of the surrounding country, fell into the hands of the Cilician pirates, whose chieftain Zenicetes occupied both cities and established his headquarters on Mt. Olympus. Under these conditions Phaselis could clearly not function as a member of the League—a state of affairs which the Lycians seem to have accepted with equanimity. Perhaps they felt that the Phaselitans were not really of themselves; at all events they apparently made no effort to expel Zenicetes. This was done, as related above, by the Roman general Servilius Vatia in 78 B.C.[1] Some time later, though not before Pompey's final suppression of the pirates in 67, Phaselis was taken back into the League, and under the Roman empire was in every way a wholly Lycian city. The personal names in the inscriptions, which down to the time of the city's inclusion in the League are exclusively Greek, from that time forward are preponderantly Lycian. Rather surprisingly perhaps, the Greek name Zenicetes continued to be used. A corresponding change was also made in the city constitution. In 300 B.C. the principal magistrate at Phaselis was the demiurgus, as in the cities of Pamphylia; in the later inscriptions this functionary disappears, and the offices mentioned are those of the League.

The pirates' activities had, however, reduced Phaselis to a lamentable state of impoverishment. As late as 48 B.C., when Pompey, defeated by Caesar at the battle of Pharsalus, made his way by sea to Phaselis, the poet Lucan calls the city 'little Phaselis', with its deserted houses and scanty populace; the citizens, he says, were outnumbered by the crew of Pompey's ship. But Lucan was never averse from a little exaggeration.

Under the *pax Romana* Phaselis, like most of the cities of

[1] Above, p. 33.

the east, has no individual history. The most exciting event of
which we have any knowledge was a visit by the Emperor
Hadrian in A.D. 129 in the course of a tour of the empire. The
Phaselitans really laid themselves out to do justice to this
occasion. Statues of the emperor were erected both by the
city and by private individuals; a fine gateway was built near
the southern harbour and dedicated to him, and a rectangular
forum was constructed, or reconstructed, in his honour. What
is more remarkable, other Lycian cities—we know of Corydalla
and Acalissus—who could not hope to be visited themselves,
erected statues of the emperor in Phaselis to greet him 'on his
landing'. Of all of this we have actual evidence in the inscriptions which have happened to survive; what else was done to
make the visit a success can only be imagined.

Distinguished citizens of Phaselis are few. The most notable
is the philosopher Theodectes, a pupil of Isocrates in the
fourth century B.C. Little is known of his philosophical views;
his chief claim to fame was his skill in propounding and solving
riddles. For example: 'There is one thing in nature whose
growth is unlike all others; when it first comes into being it is
very large, in the middle of its life very small, then again very
large as it approaches extinction.' Answer: a shadow. Or again:
'There are two sisters, the first of whom gives birth to the
second, and the second gives birth to the first.' The answer to
this one is: night and day. A statue of Theodectes stood in
Phaselis; and one evening Alexander, during his stay in the
city, roaming the streets with a party of companions after a
good dinner, noticed the statue and in a mood of exhilaration
—he was not an abstemious man—took the wreaths from his
companions' heads and threw them on the statue, thereby
paying (as Plutarch observes) a graceful compliment both to
the philosopher and to his own association with philosophy
through his tutor Aristotle.

The Roman writer Aelian, in his book on the Nature of
Animals, written about A.D. 200, says that the men of Phaselis
were driven out by a plague of wasps. He cannot mean that the
city was permanently abandoned for this reason (as Myus was
because of the mosquitoes), as Phaselis was still striking coins
in the middle of the third century; the visitation, if it really

occurred at all, can only have been a temporary inconvenience. At the same time, friends of the writer have told him that on their visit to Phaselis their pleasure was spoilt by a multitude of hornets. The writer himself has not suffered in this way on any of his three visits.

We have one other curious little item of information concerning Phaselis: the citizens favoured a special style of hairdo, which they called *sisoe*. Though peculiarly Phaselitan, this must have had a vogue elsewhere as well, for it has the distinction of being forbidden in Leviticus (19, 27): 'Ye shall not make a *sisoe* of the hair of your heads.' So the Septuagint; the English Revised Version has: 'Ye shall not round the corners of your heads.' What the authority for this rendering may be the present writer cannot say, nor whether it may be accepted as a true indication of what the *sisoe* was like; some day, when Phaselis is excavated, a statue may perhaps enlighten us.

The site of Phaselis has never been in doubt. It is identified with certainty with the ruins on the headland a little to the north-east of the village of Tekirova; the ancient descriptions suit this site well, and a dozen inscriptions found there and naming the city are conclusive proof. Ancient authors are agreed in calling the city 'lofty' and 'windy'; the cliffs are, in fact, hardly more than 60 feet high, but the headland is conspicuous and looks higher than it is. All headlands tend to be windy; but few people would think of applying this epithet to the place as a whole. In its present overgrown state it is hot and almost breathless.

The site is now quite deserted, and the ancient remains are largely lost in the tangle of vegetation. Nevertheless it has, at least for the writer, a charm beyond most others. The sleepy summer heat, the sea and the superb mountains, the contrast of the utter solitude with the busy life of the ancient city, combine to leave a memory not easily effaced. At the same time there is no denying it is not an easy place to move about in. It is also unhealthy, and was so even in antiquity. The cause of this is chiefly the marsh which lies near the isthmus and drains into the northern harbour; it is recorded by the ancient writers as a lake, and has no doubt degenerated. Livy records an occasion when a Rhodian fleet called at Phaselis; he describes the place as oppressive, and the heat and the strange smells caused an outbreak of disease among the sailors, presumably some kind of fever.

Directly behind the city rises the beautiful conical Tahtalı Dağ, 7,800 feet in height. There is some uncertainty about its ancient name. Strabo speaks of 'Olympus, a large city, and a mountain of the same name, also called Phoenicus'; then 'Phaselis, a noteworthy city with three harbours and a lake; above it is Mt. Solyma and the Pisidian city of Termessus'. Some scholars have accordingly identified Mt. Olympus with the Musa Dağı directly above the city of Olympus, and Solyma with Tahtalı Dağ. But the coupling of Tahtalı with Termessus, more than thirty miles away, is peculiar, as a glance at the map will show; moreover, Strabo in another passage, in connexion with Zenicetes, speaks of 'Mt. Olympus and a fortress of the same name from which one may look down on the whole of Lycia and Pamphylia and Pisidia and Milyas'; this was Zenicetes' stronghold, in which he burned himself and his family to death. Now, this is in any case an exaggeration; but spoken of Musa Dağı (altitude 3,250 feet) it is quite absurd. Musa Dağı commands a view of the sea and the neighbouring littoral, and on a clear day the coast of Pamphylia, forty-five miles away, may just be visible, but the rest is merely ridiculous. Spoken of the Tahtalı Dağ it is a good deal better. The present writer has never climbed this mountain, and cannot speak from experience; but at least the lower valley of the Alâkır river must be well in sight, and no doubt the plain of Pamphylia, perhaps even (always supposing clear weather) the mountains around Termessus; but further westward the view is completely cut off by the mighty massif of the Bey Dağı, more than 10,000 feet high. From the summit of this latter, on the other hand, the view is limited only by the clearness of the air and the power of the human eye. But the Bey Dağı cannot be Olympus; it is surely Solyma. Strabo gives the name Solymus to the 'crest above the peak of Termessus', and the Termessians, as was seen in a previous chapter, called themselves Solymians. Since the Bey Dağı can obviously be said equally well to lie above Phaselis, it seems most probable that Tahtalı Dağ is Olympus. Strabo does not say that Mt. Olympus is immediately above the city of that name; and having already named it when he comes to Phaselis he does not mention it a second time. The alternative name Phoenicus then remains for the Musa Dağı; like the modern Finike, it recalls the presence of date-palms rather than Phoenicians on this coast.[1] Strabo's account is still some way from being satisfactory; it is unlikely that he knew this region personally, and it seems impossible to acquit him of some degree of inaccuracy.

The three harbours mentioned by Strabo and others are easily recognised. The largest is on the south-west side of the headland, and was protected by a mole some 200 yards long, most of which is now under water. The 'petrified beach' noted by Beaufort on the west side of this harbour is not, in fact, a very remarkable phenomenon. The second harbour, B on the plan, is much smaller. Being exposed to the north and east, it needed a strong sea-wall, and this is comparatively well preserved. It abuts at each end on the shore, and in the middle on a large rock, and has a narrow entrance near its south end. The third harbour, A, is merely an open roadstead, much exposed and usable only in favourable conditions; the approach to it from the sea is impeded by rocks. On its south side are considerable remains of an ancient quay, constructed of large rectangular blocks. A channel from the swamp discharges into the sea in this bay, seeping through the sandy beach.

The mercantile activity of Phaselis that these harbours served has already been stressed; we have some information concerning the special products of the country that were dealt in. Phaselitan rose-perfume was famous, evidently a precursor of the powerful *gülyağı* which is made in Turkey today; when Beaufort was at Tekirova in 1811 he was solemnly assured that roses bloom on the summit of Tahtalı all the year round. Mention is also made of an unguent extracted from lilies. Export of dates is not unexpected in view of Mt. Phoenicus in the neighbourhood; nowadays the dates of this region are not

---

[1] *Phoenix* is the Greek for a date-palm. It remains uncertain whether Strabo's Solyma and Solymus both refer to the Bey Dağı or whether Solymus is to be distinguished as the rocky peak just above Termessus itself.

of much account. A trade in timber, the staple product of Lycia, though not specifically mentioned here, may no doubt be assumed.

The Phaselitans' devotion to commerce earned them a bad name, even in the classical Greek age, as overkeen business-men, with too sharp an eye to the main chance. Demosthenes says of them: 'They are very clever at borrowing money in the market, then as soon as they have it they forget that it was a loan, and when called on for repayment think up all sorts of excuses and pretexts, and if they do repay it they feel that they have been done out of their own property; and in general they are the most scoundrelly and unscrupulous of men.' Stratonicus' judgment that the men of Phaselis were the most rascally in Pamphylia was recorded above.[1] Another of his sayings, to similar effect, is also reported: when in Phaselis he took a bath, and was charged by the attendant at the usual price; the proprietor, however, intervened, pointing out that foreigners were required to pay at a higher rate. Stratonicus then turned on the attendant: 'You rascal,' he said, 'you came within a penny of making me a Phaselitan.' He may have had a special reason to be indignant, for at one period the Phaseli-tans, having need to raise funds, had offered their citizenship to all comers at 100 drachmae a head; many worthless elements enrolled, and Phaselitan citizenship was in disrepute.

The surface of the headland is covered with ruins of ancient houses, now heavily overgrown. The cliffs have been eroded by the sea, and as at Sillyum the halves of round cisterns are left at the cliff-edge. There are some remains of fortification-walls above the south harbour C; probably none were needed on the cliffs, but any that there may have been have now been carried away by the erosion. At M on the plan is a small building, apparently a temple, now utterly ruined, in which lies a round altar with elegant decoration and an inscription to Zeus Boulaeus; close by are statue-bases of the Emperors Antoninus Pius and Caracalla. At N is a large round cistern, carefully constructed and well preserved, with two roofing-slabs still in place.

In the west face of the hill, near the top, is the theatre; it

[1] Above, p. 80.

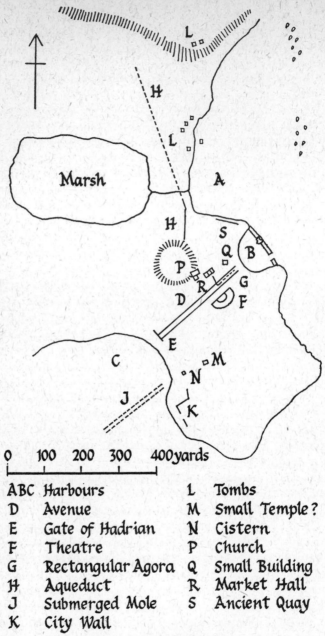

Marsh

0   100   200   300   400 yards

ABC	Harbours	L	Tombs
D	Avenue	M	Small Temple?
E	Gate of Hadrian	N	Cistern
F	Theatre	P	Church
G	Rectangular Agora	Q	Small Building
H	Aqueduct	R	Market Hall
J	Submerged Mole	S	Ancient Quay
K	City Wall		

FIG. 29 Plan of Phaselis

162

is of smallish size and much overgrown with trees. The rows of
seats are partly visible; earlier travellers counted twenty rows,
but the exact number is hardly determinable under present
conditions. The stage-building is standing in part up to the
level of the second storey (Pl. 73); its masonry is of indifferent
quality, and in the upper parts distinctly poor. It has three
large doors about 8 feet above the present ground-level; this
must have been the approximate height of the proscenium, or
stage, but of this latter there is no trace; it was presumably, as
often, constructed of wood. On either side of the middle door
is a window some 6 feet higher up; and below the large doors is
a row of four small doors which opened into the space under the
stage. Doors of this kind were used to admit animals into the
orchestra when wild beast shows were held in the theatre.
The orchestra has been dug out, probably by treasure-seekers,
below its original level.

A key feature in the layout of the city is the fine paved
avenue which leads across the neck of the peninsula. It begins
near the southern harbour at the handsome monumental gateway mentioned above, which was erected in honour of
Hadrian's visit; all that now remains of this is a jumble of
blocks and architectural fragments, including a portion of the
dedication to the emperor. From here the avenue runs straight
for some 300 yards to the shore of the small harbour B. It is
twelve paces wide between the steps which line it on either
side. Towards its north end a covered drain runs down from
the building R and turns left along the middle of the street.
Some scholars have strangely supposed this avenue to be a
stadium; it is, of course, much too long and narrow, nor could
a stadium have a paved floor. There must presumably have
been a stadium at Phaselis, as we know from inscriptions of
two athletic festivals celebrated there; but this is not it. At its
north end, between the main hill and the harbour B, is the
'rectangular agora', so described in the inscription dedicating
it to Hadrian (G on the plan); it is now quite featureless.

Across the avenue from the theatre is a low hill which seems
to have been fortified in antiquity. From inscriptions found
upon it this hill apparently carried two temples, though they
are not now to be identified. One of them was that of Athena

Polias, the chief deity of Phaselis, the other a round building dedicated to Hestia and Hermes; they date respectively from the fifth and third centuries B.C. In the temple of Athena was preserved the spear of Achilles; its point and butt were of bronze, proving, as Pausanias observes, that the Homeric heroes used weapons of bronze—which, of course, they did.

At the foot of this hill, beside the paved avenue, are the conspicuous ruins of several buildings. P is a church, with apse at the north-east end and an earlier building adjoining at the other end; fifth-century bishops of Phaselis are recorded. Q is a small edifice with a double row of unfluted columns down the middle. R is a large structure comprising three halls side by side communicating by doors, with a small apse and a door at the south end; this is perhaps a market-hall.

The aqueduct H, which brought water from the high ground to the north, leads directly to this hill, from which it was no doubt distributed to the rest of the city. The aqueduct is of the usual Roman type, supported on high arches which are still quite well preserved (Pl. 71). In earlier times, unless the water of the lake was usable, the citizens must have depended on rain-water cisterns, many of which are still to be seen; the Admiralty Chart notes a stream of good water about a mile to the south of the city.

On the shore of the northern harbour A, and on the adjoining hillside, are a number of tombs, some sarcophagi (Pl. 74), others built of masonry. One of these, under a tree by the shore, is decorated with lions' heads and a recumbent female figure lacking the head (Pl. 70). Others have suffered a good deal since they were seen by the early travellers; Beaufort mentions one with reliefs of an elephant and a rhinoceros, but it seems doubtful whether these can really have been rightly identified.

The visitor will certainly leave Phaselis with reluctance; few other sites in the writer's experience better repay the trouble of reaching them. It is, however, likely that in the near future Phaselis will become much more easily accessible, when the projected coast-road is completed. There is even some talk of an excavation. All this will make for the tourist's convenience; it is only to be hoped that the charm will not be spoilt.

CHAPTER TWELVE

*

Olympus

SOME TWENTY MOUNTAINS in antiquity are known to have
borne the name Olympus; it is likely that this is an old pre-Greek
word meaning 'mountain'. The most famous is, of course, the
Thessalian, the home of the gods, and after this the Mysian,
now called Ulu Dağ, above Bursa. By comparison with these
the Lycian Olympus is a very minor affair. In some cases the
name was extended from the mountain to the neighbouring
town; the best-known example is Olympia in the Peloponnese,
scene of the Olympic games. So in Lycia we have the mountain
—almost certainly Tahtalı Dağ[1]—and the city of the same
name some ten miles to the south.

Nothing whatever is known of the origins of Olympus. The
mountain had no doubt borne its name from the earliest times;
but the city makes its first appearance in the second century
B.C. At that time it struck coins of the type of the Lycian
League, so was evidently a member, and by 100 B.C. was
reckoned among the most important cities of Lycia. The
members of the League were divided into three classes, possessing one, two or three votes in the federal assembly, and
Strabo tells us that Olympus was one of the six which belonged
to the three-vote class. Strabo, who wrote in the time of
Augustus, had this information from the Ephesian historian
Artemidorus, so that it represents the state of affairs about a
century before his time. Of the six cities in question four are
situated in the Xanthus valley, which was the real core of
Lycia; one, Myra, represents the centre of the country, and
one, Olympus, the east.

Cicero calls Olympus an ancient city. It is doubtful how
great an antiquity should be ascribed to it on the strength of

[1] Above, p. 159.

165

this notice, and some scholars have supposed that, in fact, it was only founded in the Hellenistic period. However this may be, it seems surprising that if a city was wanted to represent the east the choice did not fall on Phaselis, an historically far more distinguished town. At the time when Artemidorus wrote Phaselis was not indeed a possible choice, for he expressly states (as reported by Strabo) that it was not then a member of the League, but had its own independent constitution. But it had previously been a member,[1] and how many votes it then possessed we do not know. Nor can we do more than guess why it had left the League. Early in the first century both Phaselis and Olympus were seized and occupied by the pirates under Zenicetes, so cannot have been effective League members then; it would be possible to suggest that Phaselis was occupied earlier than Olympus and so account for the state of affairs recorded by Artemidorus. But his statement that Phaselis was independent does not agree well with this, and it seems that there must have been some other reason for its withdrawal which we do not know.

About 100 B.C., then, Olympus is a first-class member of the Lycian League and Phaselis is not a member at all. Some years later they are both in the hands of Zenicetes, and in 78 B.C. they are both retaken by Servilius Vatia. Their territories then became Roman property, *ager publicus*, to be given, sold or leased to private individuals, and probably remained so at least until the end of the civil wars and the establishment of the empire. Strabo calls Olympus 'a great city', Cicero calls it 'an ancient city richly furnished in every way' at the time of Servilius' campaign; the occupation by the pirates undoubtedly reduced its prosperity, and Pliny in the first century A.D. actually speaks of it in the past tense, as if it no longer even existed. In this he certainly goes much too far; under the empire Olympus was again a respected member of the League. In the second century an Olympene was chosen as ambassador to carry a decree of the League to the emperor; and at that time also the citizens were celebrating periodically a great festival in honour of Hephaestus, their principal deity. Solinus' assertion in the third century that Olympus 'was once

[1] Above, p. 155.

a noble city, but has ceased to exist and is now a mere fortress' is another great exaggeration; at the time it was written
Olympus was issuing its own coins.

Plutarch, recounting Pompey's campaign against the
pirates, gives us a very curious item of information. 'These
pirates', he says, 'used to make strange sacrifices in Olympus
and celebrated certain secret rites, one of which, that of
Mithras, first introduced by them, continues in vogue to our
own day.' The cult of Mithras, the pure spirit of light in the
system of Zoroaster, was indeed immensely popular all over
the Roman empire, and in the second century is said to have
been more widespread than Christianity. There is no doubt
that it was brought from the east by the Roman legions, and
it is interesting to find the Cilician pirates, of all people,
helping to spread the cult of Mazdaism to the west.

For the rest, Olympus is noted for its high-quality saffron,
for Bishop Methodius, its only distinguished citizen, and above
all for the perennial fire which burns on the mountain close by.

This remarkable phenomenon lies some 800 or 900 feet up
in the hills a few miles to the north-west of Olympus. On foot
it is reckoned an hour and a half each way, but with a vehicle
capable of travelling over sand and loose shingle it is possible
to drive to the foot of the mountain, from where it is a short
half-hour's climb to the spot. The path is a good one, and in
several places remains of the ancient paved way are to be
seen. The fire, called by the Turks *Yanar*, has been burning
continuously since classical antiquity at least, and no doubt
since long before then, though it changes its appearance
from time to time.

As a whole the hillside is thickly wooded, but at one point is
an open space almost bare of vegetation, some 50 yards wide and
long, strewn with white and grey stones. Towards the bottom
of this the fire is burning in a deep hole 2 or 3 feet in width;
at night it is visible from far out to sea, but by day it is much
less spectacular. The flame hardly rises above the mouth of the
hole; its volume is about that of a small bonfire (Pl. 77). This
is very much the same that Beaufort saw in 1811, but other
reports vary considerably. Spratt in 1842 says that in addition
to the large flame there were smaller jets issuing from crevices

in the sides of a crater-like cavity 5 or 6 feet deep. Von Luschan in 1882 also saw one main vent and numerous small ones, and Hogarth in 1904 found almost invisible flames rising from a dozen vents. At present (1967) there is only one minor place where a gas emerges, just above the main fire on the south side; it burns only when a match is applied.

There are numerous ancient notices of the *Yanar*, and all agree that the flame cannot be quenched with water, but only by throwing earth or rubbish on it—though, of course, it will break out again. How many and how large vents there were in antiquity is uncertain; today the minor fire is easily extinguished by a small quantity either of soil or of water, and can even be blown out, and the main flame, too, will succumb to a glass of water, though it re-ignites itself in ten or fifteen seconds.

Bishop Methodius, who visited the spot about A.D. 300, says that the fire rises spontaneously from the earth in a flat place where the ground is cut up like a torn cloak; that the flame, though hot to the touch, does not consume the flesh like ordinary fire; and that the bushes grow and thrive so well around it that you would imagine they were growing beside a perennial stream. In this account only the last sentence corresponds to the present state of affairs; there is, in fact, a spring of water close by on the north.

Certain other ancient writers, as so often, sought to make the phenomenon even more phenomenal. So Pliny asserts that the neighbouring mountains, if touched with a lighted torch, will burst into flames, so that even the stones in the rivers catch fire, and that if you draw a furrow in the earth with a lighted stick a trail of fire will follow it. This is, of course, wild exaggeration; but their further assertion that water actually feeds the flame may possibly have, or have had, a grain of truth in it. At all events, Hogarth was told by his guides that fire would break out wherever water was poured, and on making the test found it to be so. Neither in 1952 nor in 1967 was the present writer able to confirm this.

Some rather uninspiring ruins of buildings stand around the fire; they represent the sanctuary of Hephaestus which stood on this spot, but themselves date from the late Middle Ages.

Hephaestus, the Roman Vulcan, god of fire, divine artificer
and husband of Aphrodite, was the chief deity of the Olym-
penes. Fines for the violation of tombs were at Olympus
commonly made payable to his temple-treasury, and the great
festival held in his honour has already been mentioned. He was
not one of the major Greek gods, and his pre-eminence
here is wholly due to the presence of the *Yanar*. Ten or twelve

Fig. 30 The Chimaera

inscriptions have been found close to the eternal fire, but not
one of them makes any reference to the fire or to Hephaestus;
they are mostly statue-bases of individual citizens.

More than one ancient author, from the fourth century B.C.
onwards, gives the name Chimaera to the mountain on which
the perennial fire burns. Now according to Homer the Chimaera was the fire-breathing monster whom Bellerophon was
set to kill by Iobates, king of Lycia.[1] He describes her as a
lion in front, a snake behind, and a goat in the middle; the
normal representation of this creature is shown in Fig. 30.

[1] Above, p. 120.

Homer does not say definitely what part of Lycia she haunted, but the later tradition located her on Mt. Cragus in the far west of the country, beyond the Xanthus valley; here, says Strabo, there is a valley called Chimaera running up from the shore. The transference of the name to the *Yanar* in the extreme east seems to be due merely to the fact that the Chimaera breathed fire; there are other examples of similar places bearing this name. One ancient commentator attempts to rationalise the matter: 'Chimaera', he says, 'is really a mountain in Lycia whose summit emits fire, with lions near by; on the middle slopes are goat pastures, and the foot of the mountain is infested with snakes'. This ingenious explanation does more credit to its author's imagination than to his knowledge of the terrain.

The nature of this wonderful fire has, of course, excited much curiosity. Its smell, perceptible only when it is ignited, has been variously compared with that of iodine, coal gas or benzine; it seems to be quite harmless. The writer, like von Luschan in 1882, noticed only a faint smell as of petrol when close to the fire. In recent years, as was no doubt inevitable, commercial interest has been aroused in the *Yanar*. Petrol is money, and Turkey is a poor country. In 1967 a team of Turkish scientists was encamped at Olympus, charged with the duty of examining the land for a considerable distance around with a view to choosing places for trial soundings. So far, it appears, analysis has revealed the existence of a small percentage of methane; the result of a fuller analysis is at the time of writing awaited. The team leader promised, however, that nothing would be done to extinguish the Chimaera.

Until recently Olympus was most conveniently visited by boat from Antalya or Finike, and this is no doubt still the most attractive approach. It is now, however, accessible also by motor transport. The road from Phaselis is very rough, but work is being done on it and it will soon be better. From Finike and Kumluca the road is quite tolerable, and some attempt is, in fact, being made to turn Olympus into a seaside resort; in 1967 two coffee-houses were installed on the beach and were doing a very fair trade. Campers should, however, be warned of mosquitoes.

The ruins of the ancient city lie at the mouth, and on either bank, of a stream which comes down from the hills to the west. This stream dries up in summer, but is reinforced by another which rises at a rock a bare half-mile up the valley and flows, in the same channel, throughout the year. It was crossed in antiquity by a bridge, of which one abutment survives; at this point the river is some 20 yards wide. It is not deep and may be crossed by stepping-stones.

On the south bank is a handsome stretch of quay wall in good polygonal masonry; the quay itself is some 5 or 6 yards wide and is backed by another similar wall still standing up to 10 feet in height. This ends on the east at a building of rough masonry which was presumably a warehouse. The polygonal masonry is of the type known as 'coursed polygonal', a style which was in vogue in the early Hellenistic period; if this dating is reliable, the city cannot have been founded much after 300 b.c. This quay now stands, at least in summer, high above the stream; moreover, the mouth of the river is closed to any possible navigation by a sand-bar. Evidently the sea-level was higher in antiquity than it is now, and boats were able to sail into the river-mouth.[1]

Also on the south bank is the theatre, small, much overgrown and in a poor state of preservation. The arched entrance on one side is, however, well preserved, but most of the seats have gone. A mound marks the position of the stage-building, but like the rest of the site it remains unexcavated. A well has at some time been sunk in the floor of the orchestra.

The main occupation was on the north bank. Close to the river-mouth is the acropolis, a small but steep hill covered with the remains of buildings; but these are of poor quality and the climb is on the whole unrewarding except for the panoramic view of the site which it affords. To the west and north-west of this lay the inhabited part of the city. The exploration of the ruins of Olympus is not for the infirm, nor to be undertaken without a guide; it is a case of pushing a way as best one can through the jungle which now covers the site. There are many remains of buildings, often standing to some height, but

---

[1] On the west coast, on the other hand, the sea-level has risen by some 5 or 6 feet since ancient times; see *Aegean Turkey*, pp. 106, 142.

they are of poor masonry and of quite unidentifiable purpose. Better pieces occur here and there, but are scarce.

On the north-west is a lake, similar to that at Phaselis, from which a small stream runs into the river. It is now an expanse of reeds, over 100 yards long, and is the main cause of the mosquitoes which infest the place at night. On its north and west sides the hills come down to the water's edge; the forest occupies the other sides.

Close to the south-east shore of this lake is the most striking monument at Olympus—a handsome door, some 16 feet high, with decorated lintel and uprights, dating probably to the second century A.D. (Pl. 75). It is built into a wall of regular smooth-faced ashlar masonry which at present ends on either side in a rough wall of small stones joined with mortar. At the foot of the door is lying a statue-base dedicated by its inscription to the Emperor Marcus Aurelius in the years 172–5. The other face of the door, towards the lake, is undecorated. This fine monument presents a problem. It appears to be the door of a large temple, and certain epistyle fragments and massive column-drums 3 feet thick which are lying near confirm this. But it stands within a few yards of the lake, leaving no room between for even a small temple. Apparently the decoration and the statue were placed, contrary to normal expectation, on the *inner* side of the door, which was entered from the undecorated side towards the lake. The writer finds this puzzling, though no other observer, to his knowledge, seems to have noticed any difficulty. In any case, nothing more of the temple appears to have survived.

The principal necropolis is on the slopes of the hill on the south side of the river. The tombs are very numerous; well over 200 of their inscriptions have been published. Most of them are of a type by no means characteristic of Lycia as a whole, namely a vaulted chamber originally covered with white plaster; in the doorways are grooves for closing the tomb with a slender door-slab. Two of the tombs, among those furthest up to the west, are inscribed, in addition to the usual epitaph, with letter-oracles. These are similar in character to the dice-oracles described above,[1] but instead of

_____
[1] Above, pp. 125–6.

throwing dice the consultant drew by lot a letter of the alphabet. The list of 'responses' consists of twenty-four lines of verse, each beginning with a different letter; some of the verses are the same on the two tombs, others are different. Here again the advice offered is virtually confined to the two alternatives: 'Go ahead' or 'Wait'. The responses are conceived as given by the heroised ancestor, and the consultants would be members of his family.

Another of the inscriptions makes the fine for violation of the tomb payable to the Chief of Police. This was a Roman official, stationed at Olympus in command of a detachment of police to maintain the peace. This duty was normally entrusted to a local force, but in places where trouble was especially likely to arise an imperial officer was sometimes appointed. In many parts of Asia Minor, as we learn from numerous inscriptions, even under the efficient government of the emperors, banditry continued to be rife. The payment of the fine to this official is, however, unusual, and looks like an attempt to curry favour.

The site of Olympus is known locally as Deliktaş, 'the Pierced Rock'. The name comes from the rock at the mouth of the river, through which passes a natural tunnel about a man's height. In Spratt's time this tunnel afforded the only passage along the shore, and he notes that horsemen normally rode round through the water. At present there is a broad strip of shingle between the rock and the sea (Pl. 76), so that even in the last century the sea-level has evidently sunk. This rock now marks the territorial boundary between the villages of Ulupınar and Yazıköy. In 1967 it was disfigured by a coffee-house at one end and an abandoned motor car at the other.

öz

Varsak

Düden Su

MA

Appendixes

Appendix I

THE SOUTH COAST CITIES IN THE DELIAN LEAGUE

WHEN THE Delian League was first formed in 478 B.C. the tribute from the allies was paid into a central treasury on the island of Delos. In 454 this treasury was transferred to Athens, and from that time for the next fifty years the amounts collected in tribute were inscribed on stone annually—or more precisely, the sixtieth part which was dedicated to Athena was so inscribed. This was the beginning of the transformation of the League into an Athenian empire. Many of the lists survive, but they are far from complete.

The south coastal cities of Asia Minor were not at first included in the League, but after Cimon's victory at the Eurymedon in 469 it was natural that they should be brought in. Plutarch says that Cimon cleared the coasts of Persian garrisons 'from Ionia as far as Pamphylia', but only in the case of Phaselis do we hear of any actual payment of money at that time.[1] Phaselis indeed continued to pay regularly from the time when the lists begin in 454 B.C.; and a single entry in 446 B.C. records that 'the Lycians and their associates' contributed ten talents. Apart from these cases there is no actual evidence for the south-coast cities until 425 B.C. The assessment list for that year includes the names, not only of Phaselis, but of Perge, Aspendus, Sillyum and even Celenderis, much further to the east on the Cilician coast. (Some of the names are only fragmentary, e.g. [P]erge, [S]illy[um], [Aspen]dus [in Pamph]ylia, but they are not really doubtful.)

Now the list for 425 B.C. is only an assessment list, not a list of actual payments, and there is no reason to suppose that any money was, in fact, collected—or indeed that the Athenians seriously expected to collect any. They had by that time lost their hold on this coast, and by 414–411 B.C. Aspendus was

---

[1] Above, p. 153.

being used as a Persian base. The only real excuse for assessing
these cities at all in 425 B.C. must be that they had earlier been
members of the League, at least in name, though we have no
record that they ever paid up. It is therefore a reasonable conclusion that Cimon's campaign in 469 B.C. did indeed have the
effect that the cities of Pamphylia were enrolled in the League.
Whether they made any actual contribution between then and
454 B.C., when the extant lists begin, we cannot know. In any
case, it is noteworthy that the name of Side, despite its importance, does not appear at any stage.

Appendix II

THE EPICYCLIC THEORY OF THE UNIVERSE

IN THE THIRD century B.C. the Greek scientists were very near to a true understanding of the solar system. Until then it was accepted belief that the earth must be at the centre of the universe, with the sun, the moon, the five planets and the fixed stars moving round it in eight concentric spheres. It was also believed, following an unfortunate pronouncement of Plato's, adopted by his pupil Aristotle, that all these bodies must move at uniform speeds in perfect circles. For the sun, moon and stars this system seemed to correspond well enough with the appearances; but the planets caused a difficulty. Their apparent speeds were obviously *not* uniform, and at times they appeared to move backwards. This was perfectly well known in the fourth century, and the problem was to account for this irregularity without abandoning the principle of circular motion at a uniform speed.

Heracleides of Pontus took the first important steps. Not only did he maintain the daily rotation of the earth, but he realised that Venus and Mercury, being always close to the sun, must be attached to the sun and revolve around it. He accordingly imagined the sun going round the earth and carrying the two minor planets spinning round it, all tracing perfect circles at uniform speed. For the two planets in question this seemed to solve the problem reasonably well.

Once the idea of motion round the sun, not round the earth, had been conceived, it was not such a long step to accept it for the other planets as well, including the earth; and this was actually done in the third century by Aristarchus of Samos. He placed the sun immovably at the centre of the universe, with the earth and the other five planets revolving round it; the earth rotated daily and the moon revolved around the earth; the fixed stars formed an immovable belt encircling the whole.

179

Here in all essentials, save only for the insistence on circular motion, was the correct conception of the solar system. But it was not accepted. The influence of Plato and Aristotle was too strong, and the earth continued to be the centre of the universe. Another explanation of the irregular heavenly motions was therefore needed, and it was provided by Apollonius of Perge and his followers. Imagine the planet to be revolving round the earth in a circular orbit, but, instead of following the line of the orbit itself, to be revolving round a fixed point on the orbit, like a point on the rim of a spinning wheel attached to the rim of a larger spinning wheel. Seen from the centre of the orbit (i.e. from the earth) its speed, though actually uniform, will appear to increase and decrease or even become retrograde. This movement of the smaller wheel is called epicyclic; it is, in fact, similar to that of the minor planets as conceived by Heracleides. If the apparent motion of the planet is still not satisfactorily accounted for, a third spinning wheel may be attached to the rim of the second, and if necessary a fourth or fifth or as many as are required. In this way almost any apparent motion can be explained. By the second century A.D. the Alexandrian scientist Ptolemy, developing this theory, had raised the number of wheels to no less than thirty-nine, and this absurdity remained canonical till the advent of Copernicus.

The ironical feature of the business is that Apollonius, who began this crazy system, was the first mathematician to study the properties of ellipses, and the motions of the heavenly bodies are, of course, elliptical. It was only necessary for Apollonius and Aristarchus to join forces, and the problem of the solar system would have been solved. But the immense prestige of Aristotle, 'the master of those that know,' was paramount throughout the Middle Ages, and all remained to be discovered over again.

(For a fuller account see Arthur Koestler, *The Sleepwalkers*.)

Short Bibliography

GENERAL

Beaufort, Capt F., *Karamania* (London 1817).
Fellows, Sir Charles, *Asia Minor* (London 1839).
Spratt, T. A. B., and Forbes, E., *Travels in Lycia* (London 1847).
Lanckoronski, Count K., *Städte Pamphyliens und Pisidiens* (Vienna 1890, in German; there is also a French edition).
Hogarth, D. G., *Accidents of an Antiquary's Life* (London1910).
Stark, Freya, *Alexander's Path* (London 1958).
Williams, Gwyn, *Turkey. A Traveller's Guide and History* (London 1967).
Antalya Tourist Bureau, *Turistik Antalya* (in Turkish, no date; a guide to the vilâyet of Antalya).

PERGE

Mansel, A. M. and Akarca, A., *Excavations and Researches at Perge* (Ankara 1949, in Turkish and English).

ALÂNYA

Lloyd, Seton, and Rice, Storm, *Alanya* ('*Ala 'iyya*) (London 1958).

SIDE

Mansel, A. M., *Die Ruinen von Side* (Berlin 1963, in German).
Mansel, A. M., *Side Kılavuzu* (Ankara 1967, in Turkish; an English translation is contemplated).

Index

Index